T0371036

MOORISH POETRY

A. J. ARBERRY

MOORISH POETRY

A
Translation of
THE PENNANTS
an Anthology compiled in 1243
by the Andalusian

IBN SA'ID

CAMBRIDGE
AT THE UNIVERSITY PRESS
1953

CAMBRIDGE UNIVERSITY PRESS
Cambridge, New York, Melbourne, Madrid, Cape Town, Singapore,
São Paulo, Delhi, Dubai, Tokyo, Mexico City

Cambridge University Press
The Edinburgh Building, Cambridge CB2 8RU, UK

Published in the United States of America by Cambridge University Press, New York

www.cambridge.org
Information on this title: www.cambridge.org/9780521170673

First published 1953
First paperback edition 2010

A catalogue record for this publication is available from the British Library

ISBN 978-0-521-17067-3 Paperback

CONTENTS

INTRODUCTION

THIS volume is a translation of an anthology of
Moorish poetry compiled in the year 1243 of the
Christian era (641 by Moslem reckoning). The author
was a certain Ibn Sa'id al-Andalusi, a native of Alcalá
la Real in southern Spain, to-day a township of some
30,000 inhabitants, lying in mountainous country to
the north-north-west of Granada, almost midway
between that city and Jaén. Born of a cultured family
and educated in Seville, he travelled extensively in
eastern Islam; the present book was actually written
in Cairo. After visiting Damascus, Mosul, Baghdad,
Basra and Mecca, Ibn Sa'id entered the service of
al-Mustansir the ruler of Tunis; later he made a second
eastern tour, and died at Damascus in 1274 (or, accord-
ing to another account, at Tunis in 1286). He wrote
a considerable number of books, the most celebrated
being a history of western Islam.

The text of this anthology, the full Arabic title of
which means 'The Pennants of the Champions and the
Standards of the Distinguished', was edited in 1942
by my eminent colleague Professor Emilio García
Gómez of Madrid. His edition, based upon a unique
manuscript, is a monument to that wide scholarship
and literary judgement which have characterized
Professor Gómez's numerous contributions to Islamic
studies, and the value of the publication is still further
enhanced by an illuminating introduction and a careful

and annotated translation. The magnitude of my debt
to his initiative is too obvious to need further elabora-
tion. If in not a few places I have differed from my
colleague in my interpretation, and occasionally in my
reading of the text, it will be appreciated by all
familiar with the peculiar difficulties of Arabic poetry
that the area of disagreement in understanding a
particular phrase or allusion is often considerable,
and I do not pretend that my alternative readings are
necessarily superior to his.

Ibn Sa'id has arranged his anthology geographically;
that is to say, he has grouped the poets according to
their birthplaces; the book falls into two main divisions,
the first part being concerned with poets born in
Moslem Spain, and the second dealing with those who
were natives of North Africa (from Morocco to Tunisia)
and Sicily. The separate geographical sections are
further subdivided according to the poets' social status
or profession. This is certainly an unusual way of
compiling an anthology, but no worse than most other
methods; it has its own special interest and value.

The author has exercised, and everywhere demon-
strates, his personal judgement, first as to the poets
selected for quotation, and secondly as to the passages
chosen. He was not able to deny himself the immodest
pleasure of quoting from his own writings, far more
extensively than from those of any other poet; and the
entire section devoted to Alcalá la Real is taken up with
the products of members of his family. This ingenuous
peccadillo should not be judged too harshly, given the
times in which Ibn Sa'id lived and the social conven-

tions then prevailing; it need not be taken as seriously impugning his literary taste, which appears in general to be of admirable refinement. In any case, he has drawn for us a singularly intimate picture of what a cultured Moor of the thirteenth century considered to be good poetry. Featured in this picture are some of the most famous writers in Arabic literature, as well as many quite obscure poets. It seems doubtful whether more than a small handful of poems have been cited in their entirety; most of the quotations are quite brief extracts—in some instances a single stanza—from what were originally lengthy compositions. In all this Ibn Sa'id is merely following the customary procedure of Arab writers on literary criticism; and the practice of citing extracts can only be explained and justified by reviewing very briefly the nature of Arabic poetry and its development down to Ibn Sa'id's time.

The origins of poetry among the Arabs are as obscure as the beginnings of Greek literature; and just as our knowledge of the latter starts with the finished master-pieces of Homer, so our record of the former commences with a number of creations already fully mature in style and language. Homer's perfect hexameters re-mained for fifteen hundred years the model of prosody in its kind, until stress replaced quantity as the measure of scansion in Greek; the various and varied rhythms discovered by unknown Bedouins at an unknown date, possibly in the fifth century of our era, conceivably earlier, have not been departed from or significantly added to down to the present time. Homer provided all later Greek writers with the legends and myths

which constitute their fabric of poetic thought, a fabric
enlarged but never even in part demolished through
the succeeding centuries. Those legends and myths had
to do with gods and heroes; they inspired sculptors and
artists not only of ancient Greece, but until this modern
age of all the western world. The myths and legends
of ancient Arabia were of a very different order; gods
and heroes do not figure in them; there is no epic story
comparable with the siege of Troy and the wanderings
of Odysseus. But if the poetry of pre-Islamic Arabia
records nothing of ancient heroes, it has much to say of
the exploits and virtues of heroic men struggling against
a harsh environment and the hostility of their fellow
desert-dwellers; and if the ancient Arabs saw no
visions of water-nymphs and dryads, they had keen
eyes for the beauty of their camels and horses, whose
excellences they never tired of describing. In the town-
settlements the Arabs also learned to value other
aesthetic pleasures, of women and wine and song.

Islam came, and with it a surfeit of warfare, and
a great surge of puritanism. The heroic myths and
legends of the desert were welcomed into the poetry of
faith; the ancient literature was eagerly collected,
and passed from oral into written tradition; it was
accepted as excellent, and taken as a model of what
Arabic poetry should be. These were the themes, and
this was the treatment; poetry acquired its grammar
and vocabulary. There were right subjects, and right
images to portray those subjects. The supremacy of
the classical poetry of the desert was the first article of
literary faith; the living poet could not go far wrong if

he memorized and strove to emulate those examples.
Then the great cities of Damascus and Baghdad revived
other less austere memories and fashions; in the teeth of
orthodox fury the myths and legends of women and
wine and song were accepted into the canon. The
vocabulary of poetic images was enlarged and enriched.

Since the themes were now specified, and their
treatment recognized, nothing remained for the
creative impulse but to vary and to refine. Poets
accordingly set themselves the task of renewing the
vitality of the old images by showing them in fresh
aspects. Critics discussed literary excellence in terms
of isolated stanzas illustrating isolated subjects. They
debated the relative importance of words and meanings
—or, as we might say, themes and treatment—as
criteria of fine composition. Precisely as Saracenic art
and architecture, denied the inspiration of the human
body, tended inevitably towards the elaboration of
arabesque ornament, the infinitely subtle variation of
geometrical design; so in Arabic poetry the business
of the creative craftsman was to invent patterns of
thought and sound within the framework of his
revered tradition. Poetry became an arabesque of
words and meanings.

All this was past history by the time in which Ibn
Sa'id lived, and it was a history to the writing of which
Arab poets living in Spain and North Africa had
contributed no small share. It was a single history
extending over the whole of the Arab empire, from
the Pyrenees to the Himalayas; the frequent travel of
men and books secured that unity of judgement and

taste which is such a remarkable feature of Arab culture. The thirteenth century happened in fact to be the point in time at which this literary movement found its culmination; thereafter for six centuries, with rare exceptions, no further development occurred; the artistic impulse was exhausted, and a terrible sterility possessed the Arab mind.

If we now look at the poetry which Ibn Sa'id gathered into his anthology, we shall recognize at once those concrete examples for which the preceding abstract analysis has been crying out. The first poem is as good a point of departure as any. The author is al-Mu'tamid, who was king of Seville from 1068 to 1091 and was thus an exact contemporary of William the Conqueror. In *Night by the River* he takes as his theme a beautiful concubine, whose attractions he depicts briefly and in conventional terms; she is compared with the bough of a *ban* tree, a species of meringa, of which the lexicographers remark that it 'grows tall, in a straight, or erect, manner, its wood having no hardness; on account of the straightness of its growth and of the growth of its branches, and their length and tenderness, the poets liken thereto the tender girl of tall and beautiful stature'. The comparison is already found in the poetry of Imrul Qais, who lived in the sixth century and is esteemed as one of the great patriarchs of Arabic literature; it is one of the commonest similes in Arabic poetry. But al-Mu'tamid develops the image and gives it new life by picturing the concubine's naked charms as a flower on the *ban* tree, now first revealed and enjoyed with the opening of its calyx, by which he represents her soft, clinging gown as it is loosened for him. The scene is enacted on the banks of a winding river; a river is not infrequently compared by the poets with a gleaming wrist seen emerging from the fringes of a green cloak; al-Muʻtamid observes that his concubine is wearing a twisting bracelet, and he therefore refines the stock image by showing both elements of the comparison together—the river itself, and the gleaming wrist adorned with the bracelet.

The second poem, *The Handsome Knight*, is constructed around the extremely stale and hackneyed comparison of a beautiful face with the noonday sun. To apply this image to a knight in battle is particularly appropriate, because the field of combat is commonly represented as being dark and shrouded in a veil of dust, and the gay and reckless demeanour of the hero facing mortal danger readily brings to mind the laughing sun. By a brilliant improvisation al-Muʻtamid likens the helmet which the handsome knight is wearing to a cloud covering the face of the sun. The cloud is said to be of ambergris, of which the best quality as the dictionaries inform us is the white or whitish; it is therefore a light heat-cloud, and indeed the gleaming steel helmet is seen to be white; a further justification for the image is the fact that the Arabic word *anbar* (amber, ambergris) is also used to denote the sperm-whale, of whose skin shields and breastplates were manufactured.

Let us pass to the single poem representing the lively humour of Habib, who was vizier of Seville in

the early part of the eleventh century and wrote a book
On the Excellence of Springtime which has survived,
to be published in 1940 by Professor Henri Pérès. *The
Wine-Bearer* is based on the interminably-repeated
comparison of the saki's blushing cheeks with the
glowing red wine; the theme occurs often enough in
this anthology, and desperately requires some variation
or other to make it acceptable once more at this late
hour. Habīb gives the image freshness with a pleasing
turn of wit; he observes that the shy young saki blushes
before the admiring gaze of the amorous drinkers, and
logically concludes that it is their eyes which have
expressed the wine in his cheeks, whereas the wine
in his flask was the produce of men's feet trampling the
grapes. The light humour of this comparison may be
usefully compared with the somewhat heavier touch
shown by Abul Hasan in his trifle *Golden Glow*, where
he pictures the reflection of golden wine on the saki's
fingers—and he uses language which recalls the familiar
likening of golden wine to the sun—as resembling the
saffron of the wild narcissus which colours the lips of
browsing cattle; this bizarre comparison, all the more
appealing to the taste of the period for its unexpected-
ness and suggestion of bathos, must surely have been
unprecedented and therefore admired for its originality.

Ibn Abdul Ghafur's *Coat of Mail* introduces us by
inversion of image to the very beautiful likening of
a river rippled by the breeze to chain armour; this
simile is so arresting when met with for the first time
that it comes as a surprise to find it one of the common-
places of Arabic poetry; this anthology contains several

extremely fine variations of the theme. The comparison is worked out in the second of the three stanzas, but the poet feels that the simile, though perfect in its normal form, is seriously defective in strict logic when inverted after the way he has in mind; he therefore protects himself from criticism by first emphasizing the invulnerability of the armour he is describing, and this he achieves through the skilful and surprising introduction of the hackneyed theme of a lover deaf to all reproaches; he reinsures against misunderstanding by adding a final stanza in which the coat of mail is shown upon the warrior's body to have indeed nothing whatsoever in common with the water to which he has likened it.

These few examples will perhaps suffice to indicate some of the ways in which the Arab poets laboured to bring fresh vitality to images faded by too frequent repetition, and the brief analyses given may assist the interested layman to find his way through that labyrinth of tortuous imagination which became more and more the dominating characteristic of creative writing; until at last the poetic genius of the Arabs discovered itself to be imprisoned and fettered to im-mobility in the impenetrable maze of its own excessive ingenuity.

Besides refining and revitalizing all these familiar and well-loved images, the poets of this period also looked to prove their originality and wit by describing scenes and sensations which had never been treated before. This was no new impulse of the Arab genius, for the old desert poets had been pleased to observe and record whatever took their fancy, and the attentive eye with which they recognized minute differences between the homogeneous features of their austere environment only needed a change of circumstance and outlook for it to see beauty and oddity in such things as a walnut, an aubergine, a thimble, a radish, an ant, or an unripe orange. Nor is it to be supposed that the flashing wit which so enlivens the sophistication of this writing was something fresh to the Arab mind; the boisterous repartee of desert life, sometimes expressed in cruel and biting satire, sometimes released in gentle and loving raillery, had predisposed the Moors to the enjoyment of humour, and the pregnant brevity of Bedouin eloquence had prepared the way for the perfect epigram.

Consider Ibn Haiyun's *Inverted Eyelids*, which must assuredly be almost if not wholly unique; very few other poets of whatever language could have attempted, or thought to attempt, such an unpromising subject, and none but an Arab could have treated it with equal delicacy and humour. The phenomenon is not uncommon in the lands of the southern Mediterranean, scourged still by a multitude of painful and disabling diseases of the eye. The poet knew that tears had often been compared in the hyperbole of passionate lyric with a flooding ocean; he was also familiar with the convention of calling the pupil the 'man' of the eye. Looking at a man suffering from this affliction, he suddenly noticed that the exposed membrane of the eye was shaped like a curved skiff; this discovery, evidence of his inventive genius, enabled him to construct a little poem of most curious charm; one can sense the delight with which he added one arresting image to another, to paint a novel, humorous, and at the same time strangely beautiful picture.

I have tried in these prefatory remarks to show, however haltingly and imperfectly, how the Moorish poet worked, and what he strove to create. These were the songs the Arabs sung, in their gorgeous palaces adorning the western provinces of their empire, in times when Europe brooded in the impotent silence of the Dark Ages. The anthology which Ibn Sa'id compiled gives us a generous selection of the poetry he knew and loved, but it is of course only a minute fraction of the enormous output of those Arabs in Spain and North Africa. It would be foolish to pretend that all the examples he quotes are masterpieces; some indeed are of very mediocre quality; but not a few are sublime. Above all, the anthology possesses the incontestable virtue of being representative, and of demonstrating authentic Arab taste; no foreigner to the language and culture could hope to illustrate the diverse aspects of this literature anything near so well by exercising his own alien judgement.

It is obviously no easy task to translate poetry so fastidiously delicate and at the same time so highly mannered; it is like trying to put Herrick and Donne into another language. The great temptation is to dilute; that I have fought my utmost to avoid, often at the expense of clarity; but I conceive it to be a part of the translator's craft to match obscurity with obscurity, and if need be bathos with bathos. Rhyme, so unfashionable in these days, seems to me absolutely indispensable to the translator of a poetry which was not only rhymed but ornamented in ways incommunicable in a foreign idiom; for rhyming, more difficult in English than in Arabic, is a necessary element of that rigorous discipline which the translator requires to save himself from eccentricity or banality.. All in all I have tried my best to write English verse mirroring as faithfully as possible (though the reflection is bound to be distorted) all the features, handsome and baroque alike, of the original poetry.

A. J. A.

Seville

KINGS

Al-Mu'tamid
(1040–95)

Night by the River

Sweet night of joyous merriment
Beside the swerving stream I spent,
Beside the maid about whose wrist
So sweetly swerved her bracelet's twist:

She loosed her robe, that I might see
Her body, lissom as a tree:
The calyx opened in that hour
And oh, the beauty of my flower!

The Handsome Knight

And when, accoutred in your mail
And with your helmet for a veil
That hid your beauty from the day,
You charged into the fray;

We deemed your countenance to be
The noonday sun, now suddenly
Occluded by an amber cloud
Its radiance to shroud.

Moon of Loveliness

She stood in all her slender grace
Veiling the sun's orb from my face:
O may her beauty ever be
So veiled from time's inconstancy!

It was as if she knew, I guess,
She was a moon of loveliness;
And may aught else the bright sun veil
Except the moon's own lustre pale?

The King's Hand

A royal hand is this
All tyrants stoop submissively to kiss:
But for its liberality alone
I had declared it Mecca's sacred stone.

The Letter

I wrote, and in my heart was burning
The grief of parting, and that yearning
They only realise
Who lose eternal paradise.

My pen no single letter traced,
But that my tears as swiftly raced
To write upon my cheek
The words my anguished heart would speak.

But for the quest of glory high
My lovesick heart were lief to fly
To thee this hour, as flows
The dew upon the waking rose.

2

The Vine

As I was passing by
A vine, its tendrils tugged my sleeve.
'Do you design', said I,
'My body so to grieve?'

'Why do you pass', the vine
Replied, 'and never greeting make?
It took this blood of mine
Your thirsting bones to slake.'

Al-Radi Billah
(d. 1091)

The Passers By

At even unexpectedly
They passed by me,
And kindled in my heart what fire
Of hot desire!

No wonder yearning pricked me so
To see them go:
The sight of waters tortures worst
The throat athirst.

Habib
(d. ca. 1050)

The Wine-Bearer

And when you passed, for all to seek,
The winecup of your blushing cheek,
Assuredly I was not slow
To quaff that wine aglow.

The tender grape is pressed below
Men's feet, to loose its precious flow;
The wine that in your soft cheek lies
Is quickened by men's eyes.

Abul Hasan
(fl. 11th century)

The Dove

Naught disturbed my tranquil mood
Save a dove, that softly cooed
On his lonely branch, supreme
Over island, over stream.

Collar of pistachio,
Throat embroidered silk aglow,
Turquoise-blue his bosom's sash,
Back and wing-tips all of ash.

Pearly lashes necklace-wise
Ringed the rubies of his eyes,
And his brow was chapleted
With a slender golden thread.

Sword-sharp was his beak, and white,
But its tip was jet as night,
Like a pen of silver dipped
Into ink, and sable-tipped.

Cushioned on his twig alone
Like a monarch on a throne,
Neck inclined, and burrowing
In his soft and folded wing.

When he saw my tears aflow
(And my weeping moved him so)
Startled, he ascended now
To the topmost leafy bough.

There his outspread wings he shook,
Clapping feathers as he took
With my heart the air, to go
Whither? Ah, I do not know.

Golden Glow

See, his slender fingers shine
In the sunlight of the wine,
As the wild narcissus tips
With its gold the óxen's lips.

Ibn Abdul Ghafur
(*fl.* 12th century)

Coat of Mail

A coat of mail, that sprays from me
The glancing shafts, as if they be
Reproaches scattered from the ear
Of lovelorn swain, too sick to hear.

5

And when I cast it down outspread
Upon the field, I would have said
Its links flow rippling o'er the net
Like rivulet to rivulet.

But when I clothe myself therein,
All emulating eyes to win
For my resolve and ardour high,
No water-armoured knight am I!

NOTABLES

Ibn al-Qutiya
(*d.* 977)

The Walnut

In its double skirt enwrapped,
Fair as aught I ever clapped
Eyes on, as when eyelids close
Over slumberful repose.

Opened to the light of day
By a dagger, you might say
'Tis the pupil of an eye
Whetted on its lid, to spy.

Inwardly it doth appear
Soft and rounded as an ear
And, to make my image true,
With its convolutions too.

6

Lilies and Roses

Drink you with the lily white
Tender in the dawning light,
Revel with the crimson rose
In the sunrise as it glows.

Each methinks has pressed its lips
Unto heaven's breasts, and sips
This the pale west's milky flood,
That the eastern pool of blood.

Comrades in rebellion
Challenging the camphor, one,
T' other bold to disobey
Justly the cornelian's sway.

One a statue, nakedly
Offered for all eyes to see,
One the cheek of lover, torn
Ruefully on parting's morn.

Or, if this my image ill is,
Pipes of silver are the lilies,
And the roses embers glowing
Fanned to flame by breezes blowing.

Avenzoar
(1113–99)

Revenge

Pillowing their cheeks all night
On their hands, now suddenly
The glow of dawning light
Surprises them, and me.

7

Ceaselessly their cups I filled,
Sucking their superfluous wine
Until my poor head reeled,
And theirs no less than mine.

So the liquor in its might
Takes revenge remorselessly:
I rocked the flask all night,
And now the wine rocks me.

In Absence

My chick, my pretty one,
My little quail, my son:
When we had to part
I left with him my heart.

I yearned so lovingly
For him, and he for me:
Bitter tears we shed
When our farewells were said.

Love must aweary grow
Of running to and fro
From thy heart to mine,
And from my heart to thine.

Drinking Song

A house well supplied,
A door ever wide,
Good wine in the cask,
A pitcher, a flask.

8

A friend of delight
To greet with the night,
His manners all charm,
His kisses no harm.

And if he deny
Or bid up too high,
The cup and the purse
Are devils, and worse!

Ibn Haiyun
(*fl.* 12th century)

Moles

My white, my shining girl,
As pretty as a pearl;
When I woo her dearly
She melts away, or nearly.

Spotted each pale cheek
With a musk-jet streak;
Beauty all excelling
There is dwelling.

I said to her, as through
My heart (and well I knew)
Her moles sent thrills of passion
In so sweet a fashion:

'Live your favours in
The whiteness of your skin,
And is that blackness token
Of hate, and my heart broken?'

9

'My father', answered she,
'A royal scribe was he;
His love so ringed about me,
He could not be without me.

'He feared that I might know
His master's secrets, so
Took pen, and in a twinkling
My cheeks with ink was sprinkling!'

Inverted Eyelids

Is a welling fountain hid
In your eye's inverted lid,
That your tears, o'erflowing it,
Run cascading through the slit?

It is curved (think I) as if
On the billows rode a skiff,
And the breeze has made it heel
Over almost to the keel.

And the man, its mariner
(So to the pupil we refer)
Fearing he may drown, no doubt,
Bales the brackish waters out.

Abu Bakr Muhammad
(*fl.* 12th century)

Panegyric

I do not know what I can bring
To court the graces of my king,
Not having any aptitude
Whereby his favours may be wooed.

Yet I will take my love for you
And consciousness of service true
To be my advocate, whose word
May likeliest in your heights be heard.

And though I lack the instruments
Of Zoar's starry eminence,
I would remind you, if you wish,
Their stars include the Unarmed Fish.

The poet was a kinsman of Avenzoar the celebrated physician and surgeon. The word Zoar (Arabic *zuhr*) signifies 'shining stars'; Abu Bakr Muhammad puns on this meaning, and describes himself also as a star, albeit the Unarmed Fish (Piscis Inermis in Virgo)—an amusing reference to the fact that he cannot claim skill in the 'instruments' of Avenzoar's surgical craft.

LAWYERS

Ibn al-Arabi
(1076–1151)

Sand

Deface not with your sand
The labours of my hand;
The breeze will be enough
To dry it with a puff.

The stuff you wish to scatter
Would mar my lovely matter,
As smallpox havoc wreaks
On beauty's tender cheeks.

This poem was composed when the author, who was Cadi of Seville, having inscribed some calligraphy a friend was about to dry the ink in the ancient manner by sprinkling sand over the page.

11

Beauty in Rags

He wrapped himself in wool,
Hoping so to fool
His friends, and came to me
Scowling dolefully.

I cried to him, 'I know
Who you are; not so
Ill saddle-cloths deface
Steeds of noble race.

'Whate'er containeth you
Seemeth lovely too;
True beauty needs not care
What it has to wear.'

The poet composed these verses when one of his students,
a handsome young man, entered his class one day dressed in
the woollen robe which was affected by Moslem ascetics.

GRAMMARIANS

Ibn al-Attar
(911–97)

White and Black

Paradise, my heavenly home
Has departed; Hell has come;
From so high felicity
See me plunged in misery!

I was bathing blithely yet
In the sun, about to set,
When behold, night's sable wing
Overshadowed every thing.

The author was swimming in a bathing-pool and was admiring a handsome white boy who was in the water. Suddenly the boy left the water, and his place was immediately taken by a negro slave.

Al-Dabbaj
(1170–1248)

Two Suns

When she floated into sight
On heaven's rim the sun was bright;
So I saw two suns appear,
The other distant, this one near.

The sun's wont, as all men find,
Is the beholder's eyes to blind;
This sun's light, I found, was a
Sure cure for my ophthalmia!

LITTERATEURS

Ibn Bassam
(d. 1147)

Mist

Hasten to your duty,
Page; none else is here
But the moon, my beauty,
And the cup, my cheer.

Hither! Be not lazy,
Seeing such a mist
Makes the meadow hazy
And the wine has kissed.

Though the garden's clouded
In a veil of tears,
It will shine unshrouded
When your sun appears.

Abus Salt
(1067–1134)

The White Charger

My white charger rode to war
Shining like a meteor,
Stepping proud and stepping bold
In his saddle-cloth of gold.

As he trotted after me
To the field of victory
Cried my rival, envious
Gazing open-mouthed at us:

'Who has bridled, if you please,
Dawn with the bright Pleiades,
Or who saddles this high noon
Lightning with the crescent moon?'

Two Seas

My noble king goes forth to ride,
A boundless sea of bounty wide;
His steed, majestic as the main,
Rolls onward, foaming to the rein;
O sight most marvellous to me—
A sea that gallops on a sea!

Arab poets commonly referred to generous patrons as
'oceans of generosity'. Abus Salt plays with this conceit.

Sun and Cloud

What a wondrous day I passed
At the Abyssinian Pool!
Heaven partly lustreful,
Partly overcast:

And the river, gently fanned
By the breezes of the glade
Shivered, like a shining blade
In a trembling hand.

The Incense Burner

Though its heart was all aflame,
Yet it never knew that same
Grief of parting, and that woe
Sundered lovers know.

When the lightning of the wine
Bathed the drinkers in its shine,
What a brave cloud billowed thence
Sweet with frankincense!

Never saw I, all my days,
Such a conflagration blaze
To persuade the revellers
Paradise was theirs.

A conflagration would normally bring to mind the torments
of Hell; the fire burning in the brazier and giving off the
sweet perfume of frankincense is thought by the poet, in
combination with the wine, to be a foretaste of Paradise.

Bounty

'Tis no matter to amaze
If thy gifts outstripped my praise,
Or thy bounty overfilled
This my vessel, ere it spilled.

Is the branch not robed in green
Long before its fruit is seen,
And must we not ring the dove
To evoke its song of love?

Al-Haitham
(*d.* 1232)

Rich and Poor

The poor are treated scurvily,
And men with unanimity
Throng the rich man's gate:
'Tis the decree of Fate.

Mankind, indeed, are likest to
Mad moths, and flutter, so they do,
Where they see the beam
Of shining guineas gleam.

Meteor

Was yon a charger, or
A flashing meteor
That passed me, blinding bright,
A levin-shaft alight?

The dawn had lent its pale
Effulgence for a veil,
Wherein (and it was apt
Indeed) he fled enwrapped.

And, as he sped, he thought
The urgent morning sought
To capture (but in vain)
Its glittering loan again.

The stars hung in the sky,
So swiftly he swept by;
The clouds in wonderment
Guessed not the way he went.

Astonishing indeed:
Though he excelled in speed
The stars, for all his haste
The dust his feet abased.

What noble prize is he
To treasure jealously;
His saddle-cloth (behold!)
Spun all of liquid gold.

Some copyist, I think,
With musk in lieu of ink
Upon his pasterns dripped
A line of manuscript.

The poet describes a white horse with black pasterns.

The Rising Sun

Behold with wondering eyes
The sun in beauty rise;
One brow is bathed in light,
One grudged as yet to sight.

As though the sun would say:
'I shall not grudge alway;
This loveliness of mine
Will soon all naked shine.'

O beauty's mirror, bare
In beauty splendid there
To east, anon to west
At even laid to rest.

The far horizons grieve
To see its radiance leave
The skies, and wrap them round
In shadows deep, profound.

And, as each star appears,
Meseems that heaven's tears
In agony supreme
Like frozen raindrops gleam.

Al-Liss
(1108–82)

The Mountain

On the sun your eyes be closing;
Strain not after Saturn's beam,
But descry yon mount, reposing
On his vanquished mount, supreme.

This verse was composed in honour of Abdul Mu'min when
he crossed from Morocco to invade Andalusia, and stood on
the conquered summit of the Rock of Gibraltar.

Night

I make complaint incessantly
Against the nights I pass in grief,
Too long when thou repellest me,
When thou admittest me too brief.

Generosity

My begging has exhausted not
Your generosity,
But is itself annulled by what
You have assigned to me.

The Thimble

'Tis like a helmet, nicked
Where thrusting lances pricked;
Some sword has dispossessed
The helmet of its crest.

19   2-2

Ibn al-Ra'i'a
(fl. 13th century)

The Fountain

The lovely fountain leaps,
Sprinkling heaven's deeps
With hurled stars, high swinging
Like a tumbler springing.

The bubbling waters glide,
A snake terrified;
The pent freshets break
Slithering to the lake.

The slow current slid
Deep in the earth hid
Till, the broad world spying,
The spray sprang, flying.

Pleased with its new berth
In sunlit earth
The fountain laughed for pride;
Lips parted wide

Disclosed teeth gleaming;
The branches, dreaming
Of love, that way and this
Swayed, the white smile to kiss.

Ibn al-Khabbaza
(*fl.* 13th century)

The Striking of the Tent

The pretender yields the crown;
See, his red tent tumbles down
When it sees red Mudar's hosts
Standing nigh, to prick his boasts.

Tell me, if you can descry:
Who has better right to high
Sovereignty—foreign churls,
Or their lawful Arab earls?

Nay, he was too negligent
Of his duty; so his tent
Wonderfully bit the dust,
And foretold the way he must.

This poem celebrates the crushing of an insurrection against
the caliph, when the Arab troops ('red Mudar's hosts')
penetrated the insurgent's camp and cut the ropes of the
pretender's red tent.

The King Who Died Young

Your life was of the order true
Of Arab eloquence;
The tale was brief, the words were few,
The meaning was immense.

Al-Kasad
(*fl.* 13th century)

The Lost Angel

That angel so adored
To heaven is restored;
Once Beauty came to birth,
But after fled from earth.

Her faithful lovers all
This day make funeral,
And in bereavement deep
Upon each other weep.

Ibn al-Sabuni
(*fl.* 13th century)

The Mirror

There's a gift of elegance
I have sent thee, this fine glass:
Let the moon of happy chance
On its high horizon pass.

Here thou canst precisely see
All thy face's loveliness,
And the sooner pardon me
The deep passion I profess.

And thou'lt find thy likeness there
Nearer to the touch than thou,
More benevolently fair,
Truer to the plighted vow.

The Red Gown

She is coming, coming,
So soft her tread,
A moon in gloaming
Rose-garmented.

As if her glances
My lifeblood shed,
And wiped their lances
In her robe of red.

Abul Hajjaj
(*fl.* 13th century)

The Reed

Behold how yonder reed
Swayed by the breath of dawn
Leans down, to sip with greed
Our glasses on the lawn.

Did not the dews suffice
Its thirst for revelling,
And does our wine entice
Its plaited locks to swing?

Towards the revellers
It shakes its graceful thighs;
The mirthful soul it stirs,
It captivates the eyes.

Come, give it that it seeks
And that our bowls possess,
And if it kiss our cheeks
Forgive its drunkenness.

23

Al-Isra'ili

(d. 1251)

The Sprouting Beard

Your cheeks were oh how fair,
How full of glowing grace
Until that sprouted there,
Your beauty to deface.

And then your cheeks became
A candle that, alack
Extinguishing its flame,
Reveals its wick is black.

Trees and Waves

Elms in the meadow springing,
Silken pennants swinging
On tawny lances;
The river dances...

Ripple of mail rises
To war; no surprise is
The elms stand steady,
Line of combat ready.

Wave on wave surging,
To the ramparts verging;
The bent elms prattle
And cry, 'To battle!'

The poet plays with the stock comparison of water rippling in the breeze with coat of mail, and develops out of this theme a picture of battle between the elms moved by the breeze and the river.

Ibn Sa'id

(d. 1274)

Invitation

Rise up! You have my leave
The flagon's seal to broach;
With stopped-up ears receive
The speech of dull reproach.

Quit abstinence (for you
Are not the first to love);
Improving thoughts eschew—
'Tis no time to improve.

See, how yon breakers white
The waters feathering
Confront the zephyr light,
A bird with outspread wing.

The river's tender side
The breeze has wounded sore;
Hark to the anguished tide
Lamenting by the shore.

The Arab poets enjoyed the conceit that the soughing of the
river against its banks was a protest against the pain caused
to its delicate flanks by the rough pebbles; it is the breeze
here which is responsible for the outrage, by blowing the
waters into waves hurrying to the shore.

Manish

'Asa the Blind
(*fl.* 12th century)

Coat of Mail

That mighty smith, the wind
Is at his task assigned;
The smooth river crinkles,
Hammered into wrinkles.

Ring by ring
The mail is fashioning;
Nail by nail the rain
Rivets the forged chain.

LAWYERS

Ibn Lubbal
(*d.* 1284)

Schooners

The schooners put to sea
How gracefully,
Horse succeeding horse
Swift to the course.

The estuary's throat
Was bare; now note
How its necklace white
Gleams in the night.

Upon their topmost spars
Lamps shine like stars,
Mirrored spears fire-tipped
In the waves dipped.

And some on paddle spring,
Some sweep on wing,
Frightened hares that slip
The falcon's grip.

The Inkstand

A servitor of learning,
In her bosom burning
A love deep-hidden
For lore both lawful and forbidden.

In night's cloak enshrouded,
Her girdle brightly crowded
With stars etherial,
The crescent moon her crown imperial.

The poet describes a silver-studded ebony inkstand.

POETS

Ibn Shakil
(*fl.* 13th century)

Ugliness

They asked me: 'Are you happy
To love her, though her teeth are gappy?'
I said: 'I am delighted
With pools that other men have slighted.

'For when, within your knowing,
Were mosses found on waters growing
Where people every minute
Come down, to dip their buckets in it?'

Ibn Ghaiyath
(1141–1222)

White Hair

They cried: 'Ha, you are hoary!'
I answered: 'What strange story!
Dawn through my darkness shining:
What cause is for repining?

'That you descry so clearly
Is no white hairs, but merely
The coursing steed of passion,
Dust-spattered in this fashion!'

The poets vied with each other in discovering ingenious
reasons and compensations for white hairs.

Algeciras

NOTABLES

Ibn Abi Ruh
(*fl.* 12th century)

Night of Joy

Turn, turn your rein
To Honey Valley,
And ask again
The while you dally

Upon a night
We two fond lovers
There passed, despite
All dull reprovers.

Her lips' sweet wine
Till dawn I tasted;
To cull her fine
Cheeks' roses hasted.

In joy extreme
We lay embracing,
As o'er a stream
Boughs interlacing.

The cups with fair
Red wine were glowing;
A cool north air
Scent-charged was blowing.

30

The garden's bloom
(Not flame-constrainèd)
So sweet perfume
Of incense rainèd.

The lamps upon
The mailclad river
Reflected, shone
Like spears a-quiver.

So there we two
Lay, till the shiver
Of spangled dew
Drove us to sever.

And in the vale,
My sad heart thrilling,
A nightingale
Was softly trilling.

MINISTERS

Ibn Ammar
(*d.* 1086)

In Praise of the King

Pass round the bowl; the breeze of morn
Is blowing free and wide,
The nightbound stars, now travel-worn,
Have tossed their reins aside.

Behold how yonder camphor, our
Great gift from rising dawn,
Gleams, as from heaven night her dower
Of amber has withdrawn.

The meadow, that fair maiden, wears
Her robe of every hue
The flowers, and a necklace bears
Bejewelled all with dew.

The roses, like some modest girl's
Shy blushes, blossom red;
The tossing myrtles hang like curls
About her lovely head.

Against the garden's gown of green
A silver wrist doth gleam:
In virgin purity serene
Flows on the silent stream.

32

Now as the breeze its surface bright
Disturbs, there seems to glow
My monarch's sword, that puts to flight
The legions of his foe.

Abbad's great son, whose bounteous hand
Alleviates all lack,
Keeps ever green the grateful land
Although the skies be black.

And he bestows, for virtue's meed,
A pure and lovely maid,
A horse of mettle and of breed,
A gem-encrusted blade.

A monarch he who, when the kings
Of earth come down to drink,
They dare not venture to the springs
Until he leaves their brink.

More fresh than dew his bounty lies
Upon the hearts of those
Who weary, sweeter to the eyes
Than slumberful repose.

He strikes the flint of ardent fame;
The fire of battle he
Quits never, save to light the flame
Of hospitality.

A king as virtuous as wise,
As charming as discreet,
A garden lovely to the eyes
With fruitfulness replete.

The Kauthar of his gifts to me
Is boundless; I know well
That with his liberality
In Paradise I dwell.

Since fruitful branches most delight,
As you observe most clear,
Their monarchs' heads you featly smite
To fructify your spear.

Observing beauty evermore
In scarlet robes arrayed
Most sweetly, with their champions' gore
Your breastplate you have sprayed.

Accept this tribute, if it please,
A garden drenched with showers
And visited by morning's breeze,
Until it bore these flowers.

I wove for their embroidery
Your fame, a golden thread,
And o'er my verses cunningly
Your fragrant praise I shed.

Who dares contend with me thereon,
Since I your name have brought
For aloes-wood, to lay upon
The brazier of my thought?

This poem is a good example of formal panegyric. In stanza
two the poet has in mind the black amber of darkness. In
stanza seven he uses the conventional simile of the life-giving
rains to describe his patron's generosity. In stanza eight he
enumerates precisely the gifts for which he is looking as a
reward for his poem. Stanza eleven mentions the two fires

the tending of which was held to epitomize ancient Arab virtue: the fires of battle and of hospitality. Kauthar which is mentioned in stanza thirteen is a river in Paradise. Stanza fifteen is an ingenious treatment of a conventional theme, the drenching of the hero's breastplate with the blood of his enemies. Stanza seventeen contains a reference to the Moorish custom of scenting the parchment on which a poem has been written. The last stanza varies this image, and is a challenge to any rival poet to excel the writer's virtuosity.

Poet's Pride

I am Ben Ammar: my repute
Is not obscure to any one
Except the fool, who would dispute
The splendour of the moon and sun.

It is no wonder if I come
So late, when time is at an end;
The glosses that expound the tome
Are ever on the margins penned.

Here the poet meets the familiar charge that all the best poetry was written long ago, and claims that a modern poet is also worthy of admiration.

Ransom

My eyes are meet and right
This page to ransom back:
Their whites against its white,
Their blacks against its black.

Spare

You criticise me, and declare
I am too wasted, and too spare:
The tempered sword is best renowned
Whose edges are most finely ground.

CIVIL SERVANTS

Ibn al-Missisi
(*fl.* 11th century)

Fragment

Praise not the avaricious man
Who gives less freely than he can;
The squinter who averts his eyes
So does, their defect to disguise.

Admire not such nobility
As stems not from an ancient tree;
The patch of white that overlays
The horse's rump is scarce a blaze!

A little bounty oft brings light
To gladden a poor beggar's night,
A tear that glitters upon some
Sick eyelid's smeared collyrium.

O who will carry to his hand
This tribute, wherein I have planned
To rain like kisses on his eyes
My rhymes, his name to eulogize?

NOTABLES

Abul Qasim
(*fl.* 12th century)

Unexpected Fortune

I met the one I loved
(But she my sickness proved),
And ventured to exclaim
A greeting in her name.

She, who so scornfully
Till then had turned from me,
Most generously now
Rained kisses on my brow.

So Moses in his days
Beheld a bush ablaze;
He sought a burning rod,
And heard the voice of God.

Moslem legend relates that Moses was seeking firewood for
his family, suffering from the cold of the desert, when he
saw the miracle of the Burning Bush.

Ibn Munakhkhal
(*d. ca.* 1165)

Dialogue

Father: Frogs are croakin'
In the valley...
Son: Words not spoken
Generally...

Father: Hear them holla
Loud and hearty...
Son: Sons of Mallah
At a party...

Father: Then their hushing,
Even stranger...
Son: Gluttons rushing
To the manger...

Father: Ne'er a prop for
Breasts a-bursting...
Son: Ne'er a drop for
Throats a-thirsting!

Ibn Munakhkhal and Ibn al-Mallah were old friends; their sons also grew up as friends, but then quarrelled. Ibn Munakhkhal reproached his son for satirizing the son of Ibn al-Mallah; they were at that time in a valley, where frogs were croaking. This dialogue then ensued.

Loule

POETS

Kuthaiyir
(*fl.* 13th century)

The Raven

The hour I saw my dear ones part
The raven, that ill-omened fowl,
Flew up, and carried in his jowl
(As so it seemed) my inmost heart.

Alone he croaked for merry cheer
In that sad hour; and why did he
With such sublime hypocrisy
In robes of mourning then appear?

The Arabs regarded the raven as a bird of ill omen for-
boding separation between lovers. The poet reproaches the
raven for wearing black wings, as if in mourning, while in
fact delighted at his misfortune.

Badajoz

KINGS

Al-Mutawakkil
(*d.* 1094)

Invitation

O Abu Talib, rise
And hasten to our view,
Then fall like morning dew
Upon our weary eyes.

The necklace that we are
Its middle gem still wants
To crown its brilliance,
While you remain afar.

CIVIL SERVANTS

Ibn al-Qabturnu
(*d.* 1126)

The Hawk

O high and mighty king,
Whose lineage doth spring
Of ancestry sublime
And pride in all its prime:

With precious favours thou
My neck hast graced; give now,
To crown thy bounty grand,
A hawk into my hand.

Let thy new offering
Be splendid on the wing,
His plumage curved and fined
In battle with the wind.

How proudly I shall stand,
A wind at my command,
And with my captive seize
The free upon the breeze!

The Party

Your friend is bidding you
Upon this day of dew
(The meadow's cheek so fair
With down new-sprouting there)

To bubbling cauldrons twain,
A melon, and to drain
With him a jar of wine,
All in a bower divine.

He could have added still
More items, did he will,
But knows how gentry hate
When friends exaggerate.

Abul Hasan
(*fl.* 12th century)

In Battle

I recalled my heart's desire
While the flames of battle darted,
And remembered how love's fire
Burned my body, when we parted.

As the foemen shaft on shaft
Thrusted, I descried her glances
Gleam among them, and I laughed
Running to embrace their lances.

POETS

Ibn Jakha
(*fl.* 11th century)

Serpent Curls

And when upon the morn
We halted, soon to part,
My spirit grew forlorn
And sorrow filled my heart.

Within the litters high
Bright moons I did behold,
Their brows encircled by
Fine veils of woven gold.

And there, each veil below
A serpent crept, to seek
The blushing rose aglow
In every tender cheek.

No malice did they bring
Upon those cheeks they pressed,
But with their cruel sting
They pricked my anguished breast.

Ibn al-Bain
(*fl.* 11th century)

Virgin Earth

The earth's a virgin fair,
The raiment of the spring
Her robe, the flowers there
Her jewels glittering.

Storm

Methinks the swooning air
Loves too my maiden fair,
And like her languid swain
Is racked by cruel pain.

The quivering lightnings dart
In his complaining heart,
And as he weeps for woe
The rains, his teardrops, flow.

And since the maid is proud,
The lover humbly bowed,
The heavens weep this while,
The shining blossoms smile.

LITTERATEURS

Ibn Abdun
(*d.* 1134)

Fate

May Allah pardon us
Our stumblings! Treacherous
The hand of Fortune proved,
The nights we laughed and loved.

Fate flatters to deceive,
Rejoices but to grieve;
A serpent's in the bloom—
We gather to our doom.

Poor Lodgings

O thou exalted mightily
On either line of ancestry,
As in a bowl the bubbles rise
Successively to kiss the skies:

The lodge wherein thy servant dwells
In no particular excels
Loved Salma's lodgings at Dhul Khal
Where desolation covers all.

When he beheld them, tumble-down,
He hailed his lodgings with a frown:
'*Good morrow to you, and good day,*
Poor ruins crumbling to decay!'

The ruins, knowing well to speak,
Responded with a plaintive squeak:
'*What glad good morrow can there be*
For veterans as worn as we?'

Command the churl who billets us
To be a bit more generous;
The fellow is a raving fool,
And cannot even work to rule.

The poet makes a semi-humorous protest against the poor lodgings in which he has been billeted, and requests the caliph for better treatment. The lines in italics are quotations from an ode by the celebrated pre-Islamic poet Imrul Qais.

Lisbon

NOTABLES

Al-Tulaitili
(*fl.* 12th century)

The Ant

Slender her flank,
Narrow her shank,
Carved to design
Exceedingly fine.

Ethiop-hued,
Lugging her food
Gripped between claws
Like a pincer's jaws.

Look at her rump:
A little lump
Of blackness, which
Is new-dripped pitch.

Or you may think
It's a blot of ink,
The hasty smudge
Of a learned judge.

Ibn Muqana
(*fl.* 12th century)

Dawn

Dawn is rising bright and clear,
Yonder see its shine appear:
Pour me wine, and quickly, ere
Sounds the solemn call to prayer.

As the wine is mixing now
Pearly bubbles wreathe its brow,
Sprinkled jewels, glittering
As they float, a liquid ring.

Let me drink with lads of breed,
Noble all of birth and deed,
Interchanging as they sit
Merry tales of spicy wit.

Other wine they quaff as well
From the cheeks of a gazelle
Blushing sweetly, and therein
Blooming rose and jessamin.

Miracles his beauties seem
All unclouded as they gleam,
Locks of jet, sublime to see
On that brow of ivory.

Lissom bough (oh what amaze!)
On a rounded hillock sways,
Night of loveliness divine
Overshadows morning's shine.

47

The soft pinion of the air,
As we pass the winecup there
Hand to hand, bedews the lawn
With the rose-water of dawn.

See, the white narcissus sips
The sweet fragrance as it drips
Flowing gently from the skies,
Teardrops spilled by lovers' eyes.

Now the Pleiades submerge
On the far horizon's verge,
Shaking out their silver shower
Like a jasmin-twig in flower.

Night's deep shadows are withdrawn
From the pallid cheek of dawn
As some crow, that skyward springs,
Shows the eggs beneath her wings.

As the sun mounts up the sky
Dazzling the beholder's eye,
There ascends thy aureole,
Prince of every faithful soul!

Santa Maria

LAWYERS

Abul Fadl
(*fl.* 12th century)

Body and Soul

Here the river's body flows,
Here stand the trees;
Breathes the river's soul, when blows
The meadow's breeze.

When the breeze unstirring lies
A sword shines there,
But a coat of mail, when sighs
The woodland air.

CIVIL SERVANTS

Abul Hasan
(*fl.* 12th century)

Revel

The brightest night of all
The nights that I recall
Was that I never ceased
Upon the wine to feast.

And as I strove to keep
My eyes apart from sleep,
To the cup's ear-ring I
Still kept its anklet nigh.

POETS

Ibn Sara
(*d.* 1123)

The Youth

See, his beard is sprouting yet,
Beauty's fringes delicate;
Delicately through my heart
Passion's thrilling raptures dart.

It is not that, so to speak,
Blackness covers up his cheek,
But his eyes have sprinkled there
Of their blackness on its fair.

Oranges

Yonder stands the orange-tree
Showing off its fruits to me,
Gleaming teardrops lovers shed
Stained by passion's heartbreak red.

Balls of agate carmine-bright
Hung on boughs of chrysolite,
Sent a-spinning from the trees
By the mallet of the breeze.

Now I kiss them, now inhale;
Thus my senses I regale
With their cheeks' so tender bloom
And the sweets of their perfume.

50

Aubergines

Fine to taste they are,
Smoothly globular,
Fed by the sweet brook
In their shady nook.

Fronds at top and toe
Clutch them round, as though
They are hearts of sheep
In the eagle's grip.

The Quince

There is nothing in the quince
That needs cause a man to wince;
What's the reason that you doubt it?
Entertain no fears about it.

Spell it slowly at your ease,
Forwards, backwards, as you please;
E C N I U—why Query
Such a comfort for the weary?

In the original there is a clever word-play on the Arabic
for quince, which I have attempted frigidly to imitate.

Fire

Fire, the daughter of the flint:
In the furnace see her glint,
Like the planets burning bright
In the shadows of the night.

Pray inform me, if you can
(Do not lie to me, my man!)
Does she have a high degree
In the art of alchemy?

So I think; for when the breeze
Howls at midnight through the trees,
Then she dances up and down
Madly in her scarlet gown.

The Benefactor

And when the travellers by night
Began his praises to recite,
And through the dusty desert spread
The scent of musk beneath his tread,

I knew from that fair eulogy
How fair is his philanthropy,
As green and verdant banks disclose
The river that between them flows.

Cordova

KINGS

Al-Mustazhir
(*d.* 1024)

The Banished Lover

All too long the night
Drags, and wearily,
Since you take delight
Thus to banish me.

Treacherous gazelle,
Mistress of delay
In your troth, and well
Tutored to betray:

Have you lost to mind
Those delightful hours
You and I reclined
On a couch of flowers?

And the stars above
Seemed like pearls to be
In an ocean of
Lapis lazuli.

Al-Nasir
(fl. 10th century)

Royal Pride

Are we not the progeny
Of Marwan, however Fate
Plays with us despitefully,
And whate'er our present state?

When the issue of our thews
Is proclaimed in royal birth
Pulpits tremble at the news,
Joy possesses all the earth.

Al-Taliq
(d. 1009)

Saki

Slender bough a-swing
On a swelling dune,
Fruit of flame a-swoon
My heart gathering.

Curling tresses slide
O'er his cheeks: behold
Over silver, gold
Streaming liquified.

Perfect loveliness
Dwells upon his brow;
Lovely is the bough
In his leafy dress.

Aureate the cup
In his fingers gleams;
Over dawn meseems
Day is mounting up.

Wine, the sun, swings high
Westward to his lips,
And his finger-tips
Frame its eastern sky.

Down his throat it flows
To the sleep it seeks,
Leaving in his cheeks
Sunset's flaming rose.

Al-Asamm
(*fl.* 12th century)

The Unripe Orange

Little daughter of the grove,
Whom the rainbow leaned to kiss
Leaving on her this and this
Gleaming token of his love.

Wondrous spectacle to view,
Hither shining purest gold,
Thither brightest emerald,
Fashioned by the dripping dew.

Moses, God's apostle, lit
Here a flame, yet brightly seen;
Khadir of the mystic green
There his hand laid over it.

As Moses was famous because of the Burning Bush, so
Moslem legend celebrated the mysterious prophet Khadir
as 'the man in green'.

Excuses

Forbear, my love,
To scold me so
That I should rove
In haunts so low.

The meanest lair,
Howe'er it stank,
Would not impair
My faith and rank.

The sun, methinks,
Still rules sublime,
Although he sinks
In mud and slime.

These verses were addressed ingeniously to the prince's wife
when she reproached him for resorting to low haunts.

Ibn Hamdin
(*d.* 1151)

Ebony and Ivory

I just beheld a monstrous crow
Squat on a lily: that, I know,
Forbodes a year (good God, defend us!)
Of sheer calamity stupendous.

Collyrium-pin of ebony,
Behave with greater dignity!
You, ivory collyrium-needle,
Be more submissive—learn to wheedle!

A negro and his white wife quarrelled before Ibn Hamdin's
tribunal, and he composed these verses for their benefit.

56

MINISTERS

Al-Mushafi
(d. 982)

Pearls

When she spoke to me
'A pearl has dropt!' I cried, and hastened
As if I would see
Whether her necklace was unfastened.

She was hushed awhile;
Then with derisive laughter pealing
Flashed on me a smile,
Another row of pearls revealing.

Ibn Hazm
(994–1063)

Mutability

Let not my jealous foes
Exult in my disgrace,
For Fortune comes and goes
Nor tarries in one place.

A free man is like gold
Now cast for hammering,
But presently, behold!
A crown upon a king.

Absent Friends

If now, as is too true,
My body's far away
My heart abides with you
For ever and a day.

But he alone knows bliss
Who looks on his adored,
And Moses prayed for this
That he might see the Lord.

The poet refers to Moses' prayer to see God as recorded in
the Koran.

Slander

They chide at me, and say
My love is sickly slender;
But I will not obey
The sly reproofs they tender.

Will not the bough whereon
The sun is ever shining
Be very apt anon
To wither and be pining?

Abul Mughira
(d. 1046)

Moon and Venus

When my eyes descried thee
In the dawn, O crescent
Moon, and close beside thee
Venus incandescent,

58

To my mind observing
Like a ball was Venus,
From thy mallet swerving
Soon to spin between us.

Ibn Burd
(d. 1053)

Daybreak

When that huge serpent, night,
Coils up, and morning's light
Illuminates the sky,
I fancy to descry

A black mosquito-net
By careless fingers set
A-blazing, as they seek
To light a lantern's wick.

Moon in Mist

The Moon, that mirror bright
Now gleams with dimmer light;
The Virgin's playful breath
Its lustre tarnisheth.

Night's vague, ambiguous waste
In its pale shine embraced
Is some dark rigmarole
Inked on a parchment scroll.

Blue and Gold

He came arrayed
In an azure gown,
All washed down
With golden braid:

A moon agleam
In a lapis sky,
Bordered by
The lightning's beam.

Ibn Zaidun
(1003–70)

Cruel Masters

Jahwar's sons! Your tyranny
Sets my spirit all ablaze;
Shall my songs still fragrant be
With the odour of your praise?

What, do you suppose that I
Am as ambergris, and doomed
On your brazier to lie
That my breath may be perfumed?

Flirtation

It is as though we never flirted
That night, with only union near us,
When luck the prying eyes averted
Of those who sought with lies to smear us.

Two secrets in the mind of darkness
Concealed from sight, we lay reposing
Until dawn's tongue with brutal starkness
Wellnigh our secret was disclosing.

Fidelity

Be proud—I'll bear with you;
Delay—yet I'll endure;
Exult—I'll grovel still;
Run off—I will pursue;
Speak—I shall hear for sure;
Command—I'll do your will.

Abu Yahya
(*fl.* 13th century)

Bloom of Age

They scold, that I engage
In love and toping, now
That the white bloom of age
Is shining on my brow.

The bough most sorely then
Requires refreshing showers
That very season, when
It wears its gown of flowers.

The Moth

The moth a merry caper
Around my flagon turned,
Supposing it a taper
That in the shadows burned.

With beating wings he hung him
About the flame I shed,
Until the flagon flung him
Upon the carpet, dead.

NOTABLES

Ibn Shuhaid
(992–1034)

Stolen Pleasure

She sprawled on the border
In drunken disorder,
Slumbering deep;
The watch was asleep.

Seeing her lie there
So close, I drew nigh there
As a friend might approach
A petition to broach.

Silently creeping
Like slumber (she sleeping)
Climbing came I
As soft as a sigh,

Kisses to tender
Her throat, white and slender,
Sweetly to sip
The dark wine of her lip.

I tasted at leisure
A nightful of pleasure,
Till o'er the lawn
Flashed the laughter of dawn.

Rain and Lightning

Mouths half-open, in their shrouds
The parched blossoms
Pressed their lips against the clouds'
Brimming bosoms.

Then the rains in majesty
Enfiladed,
Abyssinian soldiery
Golden-bladed.

Sword and Lance

The sword is a sheathed rivulet, to whose brink
Death comes to drink,
The lance a bough, that drips a crimson flood
And fruits in blood.

Ibn Abdus
(*fl.* 11th century)

A White Horse with a Crimson Flash

There's a handsome steed,
Splendid as his breed;
Flame upon his back—
He's no piebald hack!

Daylight o'er him shone
Claiming him her own,
And the twilight there
Stole her crimson share.

Ibn Quzman
(*d.* 1160)

The Radish

The radish is a good
And doubtless wholesome food,
But proves, to vex the eater,
A powerful repeater.

This only fault I find:
What should be left behind
Comes issuing instead
Right from the eater's head!

Abu Amr
(*fl.* 12th century)

Bad Company

Avoid the friend who's parasitic
(Like certain particles enclitic)
And loves to be, like Amr, a ranger
Betwixt compatriot and stranger.

Bad company is most contagious;
As proof of its effect outrageous,
The spear that in bad blood keeps dipping
Shows on its point with what it's dripping.

The second line of the first stanza reproduces a frigid grammatical joke in the original, a not infrequent characteristic of poetry of this period. The author was a son of Ibn Hazm, quoted earlier in the anthology, who wrote *The Ring of the Dove.*

Siraj
(*d.* 1114)

Nightfall

When I see the life of day
Ebbing fatefully away,
Night approaching, all sublime
In her fresh and youthful prime,

And the sun leans down, to spill
Saffron over every hill,
Over every lowland dusk
Scattering her grains of musk,

Then I bid the cup arise
Like a moon into your skies,
Where as Mercury you reign
Over all your starry train.

The House of the Heart

When he entered on my heart,
Taking it to be his dwelling,
And authority compelling
To his eyes to impart;

Then his mercy I besought,
Sighing so for his compassion
That I told him, in such fashion,
My most secret thought.

'Have a care! More gently come
To this lodge you are enjoying;
Are you bent upon destroying
With your hands your home?'

Benevolence

Broadcast widely if you can
The beneficence you plan,
Troubling not if near or far
Its receiving stations are.

So the rain has little care
What it falls upon, or where,
Irrigating equally
Barren rock and fertile lea.

Abu Ishaq
(*fl.* 12th century)

Changefulness

My friends, reproach not me
With mutability
Because the singer's art
Ensnares and traps my heart:

Now frozen, cold as snow,
Now joyous and aglow,
As pliant ash will suit
Alike the bow and lute.

Abu Hafs
(*fl.* 12th century)

Beauty

Upon her eyes they gazed,
And they were sore amazed;
All wine-consumers find
How wine consumes the mind.

Her glances all men dread,
But she still keeps her head;
The bearer of the blade
Needs not to be afraid.

My eager eyes upleapt
To greet her, and I wept;
The clouds, that swim below
The sun, with rain o'erflow.

I weep, when I recall
Her stature slim and tall;
Upon his bough the dove
Sighs his lament of love.

She left me, and my breast
A sombre grief oppressed;
At sunset over all
The world deep shadows fall.

Hips

Her hips, so wide-distended
From her slim waist suspended
Exert their tyranny
On her as much as me.

I think upon their treason
And suffer in my reason;
And she has aching thighs
When she attempts to rise.

5-2

Sunburn

Friend: The sun's relentless hand
Its burning light has cast
On you, and left a brand
That never moon surpassed.

Poet: But, recognizing now
The havoc that he wreaks,
He lowers his pale brow
And my forgiveness seeks.

SCHOLARS

Ibn Iyad
(*fl.* 12th century)

The Glance

Her glance denied to me
It acted vengefully:
Was ever bright sword seen
Without its edge was keen?

And so, when I descried
How she contrived to hide
And strict seclusion kept
Behind the tears I wept,

I flaunted to my love
My river and my dove—
The first, my weeping eyes,
The second, my sad sighs.

Beardless Youth

A lustrous face,
My lovely gipsy's,
Whose sun no trace
Of moss eclipses.

Ibn Maimun
(d. 1171)

Immunity

I adventured fearlessly
In love's flame that fired my breast,
Boldly plunged into the sea
From my weeping eyes expressed.

Am I Father Abraham
That such blaze I could endure?
Is it Moses that I am
That from drowning I'm secure?

The Koran relates how Abraham was flung into a fiery
furnace by the tyrant Nimrod, but God miraculously
delivered him from the flames. Moses was preserved from
drowning in the crossing of the Red Sea.

Ibn Abd Rabbihi

(860–940)

Modest Blush

Never, never did I see
Neither have I heard the same,
That a pearl can turn for shame
Into red chalcedony.

When you gaze with awe profound
On the beauty of his brow
Lo, you see your beauty now
In its liquid lustre drowned.

Favourites

O you, who on your cheek
Have drawn two lines of down
That wild disorder wreak
And panic all the town:

I never knew your glance
Was such a cutting blade,
Till you appeared by chance
In your down-thongs arrayed.

The Arab poets were fond of comparing the favourites
affected by a handsome youth with the shoulder-belt on
which the sword would be suspended—the sword being in
this case the sharp and wounding glances of the beloved's
eyes.

Ritual

Pretty as a posy
Runs my maid divine,
In her fingers rosy
Bearing rosy wine.

See with what devotion
Ewer bows to glass;
Prostrate to the potion
Kneels my godless lass.

Jasmin's silver scatter
Wondrous to behold:
Jonquil's golden platter
Stemmed on emerald.

Al-Ramadi
(d. 1022)

The Shaven Beauty

They have shaved his head
In ugliness to dress him;
They were full of dread,
And jealous to possess him.

Black as night, and bright
As dawn, until his shaving,
Now he's lost his night,
Thank God his dawn still saving!

Ubada
(d. ca. 1030)

Drinking Song

Hasten hither, saki mine,
And deflower the virgin wine;
Take my silver (nay, be bold!)
And convert it into gold.

Let the drunkard (hark to me!)
Firmly grasp this recipe
In his fingers, and in truth
He shall find eternal youth.

Ibn Baqi
(d. 1145)

The Champion

He has soared to the crest
Of attainable glory:
No other can fly with him.
He arose in the West—
East, show in your story
A hero to vie with him!

Bacchanal

As o'er the world came trailing
The silent skirts of dusk
I poured her wine, exhaling
The tender breath of musk.

72

I grasped her, as caresses
The warrior his sword;
Her harness was the tresses
That o'er my shoulder poured.

And when, o'ercome by slumber
She leaned on me to rest,
I stirred, to disencumber
My bosom of her breast.

I yearned to hold her to me,
But put her from me thus
Lest she be pressing, through me,
A pillow tremulous.

Love's Evidence

If my tears desert me, why
Do they slyly wink, and cry
'He has consoled him', or
'He did not love before'?

Will they not believe my sighs
Rather than my barren eyes,
As, when laments the dove,
They say, 'He sings of love'?

Anonymous

Sleep

Sleep, darling, stayed
On my bosom leaping,
Like a baby sleeping
In a cradle swayed.

73

Ibn Kharuf
(*d.* 1205)

Aleppo

I have milked well the breast
Of Fortune, tasting each extreme;
Aleppo I love best,
For there alone I found the cream.

The poet puns on the Arabic name for Aleppo, which is
closely similar to the word for milk.

The Dancer

As his movements twist and wind
He plays havoc with my mind,
Lightly tossing off his dress
To be robed in loveliness.

Now he writhes with supple ease
Like a bough before the breeze,
Gambols now as a gazelle
In its covert on the fell.

Now retreat, and now advance:
How the reason he enchants,
And upon the feelings plays
As does Fortune with our days.

Now he lithely screws his feet
Till upon his head they meet,
As the tempered sword will bend
Till its handle grasps its end.

The Tailor's Apprentice

Sons of Mughira! I love well
Among your tribe a young gazelle;
Your lances' shadows guard him so,
He needs not to his thorn to go.

His stool, the steed he rides upon
Rejoices in its champion
Armed with the needle that he plies
Sharp as the lashes of his eyes.

The needle o'er the silken dress
Careers with wondrous nimbleness,
As down the sky bright meteors snake
With threads of lightning in their wake.

Wages

The dawn of my intelligence
Is risen fair and bright;
The dimming planets of my pence
Have vanished out of sight.

If the dark night of ignorance
Had compassed me about,
Gold guineas in full radiance
Like stars would have shone out.

Toledo

SCHOLARS

Al-Assal
(*d.* 1094)

Toledo Captured by the Franks

Men of Andalus, to horse!
Mount your steeds and swiftly ride;
It were an erroneous course
Longer here to abide.

Garments ordinarily
By their fringes are divested;
Our imperial robe I see
From the middle wrested.

POETS

Ibn Billita
(*d.* 1048)

Dawn

Darkness' Ethiop soldiery
Are routed now, and flee;
Dawn has loosed his Coptic horde
To put them to the sword.

Drunken Beauty

He reeled, intoxicated:
Yet I could not have stated
Whether with beauty's pride,
Or with the liquor's tide.

He came, my drunken vagrant;
His nectared breath was fragrant
As with sweet basil's scent
At nightfall redolent.

Upon his cheeks white-gleaming
His moles cast shadows, seeming
Like hours of sadness spent
In passion's banishment.

Marguerite

Shining marguerite,
Flower fair and sweet,
Golden glow a-glimmer
On your silver shimmer.

Frankish slave, pale-faced,
Magian faith embraced,
Mystic fire discerning,
To its altar turning.

Mouth of my adored,
And, for love's reward,
Gleaming gold I shower
In her mouth, my flower.

Sails

A skiff I spied
Swimming lazily;
I watched it ride
On the idle sea.

A bird it seemed
To my wondering view;
Its spread wings gleamed
White upon the blue.

Al-Hajjam
(*fl.* 11th century)

The Candle

The burning candle glows
Bright as yon Pleiades,
Fresh-kindled by the breeze
As it softly blows.

A serpent's tongue it seems
That flickers in the glow
Of the hot noontide; so
Quivering it gleams.

The Stork

She comes, an exile fair
In flight, to bear
Glad tidings on her wing
Of joyous spring.

Spread wings of ebony,
Clapped ivory,
Squawked laughter loud and good
Of sandal-wood.

The wings of the stork are seen to be black, and white
underneath; its beak is yellow as sandal-wood.

Vultures

The dead lie strewn about
Like stones; the vultures dart
To pluck their vitals out
And rend their ribs apart.

All crimson with the meal,
They look as though they were
Old women, who aneal
With henna their white hair.

The Broken Water-Wheel

Singing as she dips,
No word upon her lips;
Every thirsty lad
Salutes her, and is glad.

Suddenly a fin
Flies off, and stops her spin
The twinkling of an eye,
Then sends her swinging high.

Like a songstress she
Who breaks her melody,
Straining at the pause
To catch the sighed applause.

The Toothpick

Why does the king not pay
Attention to my plight,
Who brightened with my ray
So long his weary sight?

Am I a toothpick then
Which, bringing into play
Their teeth to whiten, men
Fling carelessly away?

False Friend

I had a friend, but he
Was no true friend to me;
A wound he was, that tore
My heart, and pained me sore.

He gloated to espy
Me slip, then like a fly
He swooped, rejoiced to sting
My ulcer festering.

The Pen

Fairer is the manuscript
When the reed is clipped;
Clearer runs the message, when
There's a trimming of the pen.

Dimly burns the lantern; but
When its wick is cut
Perfect will its lustre be
Through the wick's deficiency.

80

Granada

KINGS

Ibn Adha
(1098–1145)

On Taking Up a Humble Place at Court

We are crescent moons, whose light
Banishes the shades of night;
Wheresoe'er we sit, we bring
Glory to the gathering.

Fate, the traitor, may efface
Wrongfully our pride of place;
Fate may take our most; yet whole
Still abides our pride of soul.

MINISTERS

Ibn al-Imam
(*fl.* 12th century)

Hopes

Human hopes are ever
The deceitful quiver
Of lightning, the entrancing
Delusive mirage dancing.

Shall my weary horses
Down the long water-courses
Evermore be roaming,
Or at last come homing?

Every day another
Lodging, a new brother,
Noontide's shade diverting
All too soon deserting.

LAWYERS

Ibn Atiya
(1088–1147)

The Night Traveller

Many a night far-faring
Along some desert vale,
My sword well-girded wearing
The shadows' skirts I trail.

Lost stars in the dreaming
Sea of darkness drown;
Lightnings flash, the gleaming
Borders of night's gown.

Night is an unsleeping
Ethiop warrior,
His wounded shoulder dripping
With the throbbing gore.

Ibn al-Faras
(1130–1200)

Moon of Beauty

She came in beauty beaming,
Like a full moon gleaming
Her face, beneath the veil
Of dusk approaching, pale.

She came, serene and stately,
The veil so delicately
Drawn above her brow,
No veil was there, I trow.

I deemed her veil the shimmer
Of waters pure, a-glimmer
Therein, for all to see,
Truth's naked purity.

Ibn Malik
(1163–1249)

Algeciras Seen Over a Stormy Sea

At Ceuta I cast aside
The saddle of my roaming,
And hoped a smoother tide
Of fortune might be coming.

My covert I did see,
Far Algeciras city;
The waves prevented me
To hunt her fawns so pretty.

As in a mirror clear
A lovely face with rapture
Is glimpsed so near, so near,
Yet so far to capture.

Sister Sun

In the dawn's first light
She shone upon my view
Shaking from her white
Brow the shimmering dew.

I cried, 'The sun I fear
Our secrets shall betray':
'Shall my sister dear
Betray me? O nay, nay!'

POETS

Ibn Hani
(*d.* 973)

Aubade

Wonderful night, that sent to me
And you a black-tressed messenger,
What time we watched the Gemini
Pendant in the ears of her!

And our saki all the night
Launched against the shadows grim
His lantern, red as dawning light,
Never extinguished, never dim.

84

Softly humming, cheeks aglow,
Slender his stature, slim and fine,
Thick-lashed eyelids, drooping low
With the burden of the wine.

The brimming liquor, tremulous,
Scarcely leaves him with a hand;
So constantly he bows to us,
Scarcely has he strength to stand.

They say, 'He is a lissom reed
Waving on a sandy dune';
Know they not a dune indeed,
Do they forget a reed so soon?

For our bed, to couch us in,
The garments of the wine we take;
The harsh shadows tear its skin
Our warm coverlet to make.

Passionate heart to passionate
Heart draws nigh, and lip to lip
Presses; for hearts are yearning yet,
And mouths would honeyed kisses sip.

I beg you, rouse his idle cup
And bid his sleepy eyelids wake;
The drowsy flagon tumbles up,
Mindful our dry throats to slake.

Darkness has already snapped
A stretch of his constricting chain;
Night's army stands to order, apt
To contend with dawn again.

The stars that crown the Pleiades
Turn their backs on all the land
And vanish; gleaming rings are these
On fingers of a hidden hand.

And in their wake Aldebaran
Lumbers on his plodding way
Like a laden journeyman,
Whose beasts are spirited astray.

Yonder shining Sirius
Advances with more urgent stride,
Spurring on impetuous
His steed Mirzam at his side.

And his sister from behind
Ere the rising of the day
Hurries to him, to unwind
Their veil that is the Milky Way.

She fears the Lion's dreadful roar
As he flashes through the night,
Nathra, his muzzle, thrust before,
And rends the darkness at a bite.

Yet, it seems, the Fishes Twain
Swimming broadly down the sky
Make to clutch him by the mane,
And undertake that he shall die:

One, the Lancer, aims his dart
And strikes, until his lifeblood drips;
Unarmed, the other in his heart
Raging, gnaws his finger-tips.

Ursa's stars, methinks, are roes
Of Wajra, searching till the dawn
A wide wilderness, where those
Seek their lost and straying fawn.

And Canopus on the rim
Of his horizon, torn apart
From a loved friend, finds after him
No other, to console his heart.

Dim Suha, that wasted swain
With his visitors, this night
Now is visible, again
And again is lost to sight.

Aloft the Pole-star, cavalier
Supreme, with pennants twain arrayed,
Very scornful seems to peer
At the stars' slow cavalcade.

Aquila, his pinions clipped,
Drops vertiginous through the skies;
His wings, no more feather-tipped,
Fail him, and he cannot rise.

His brother, wheeling yet on wing
Sublime, unwearied to the prey,
Suddenly appears to spring
And snatches half the moon away.

Night, circumferenced in profound
Darkness, black as ebony,
Presently is swathed around
In purple weave of majesty.

As her shadows now decline
Swaying slantwise o'er the earth,
Meseems she passed the night with wine
And staggers in her drunken mirth.

Dawn, lifting up his pole of light,
Is a Turkish monarch, who
Challenges that Ethiop night,
And he vanishes from view.

The sun's standard fluttering
Is Jaafar, my Lord-Emperor
Who, looking on a rival king,
Only laughs, and laughs the more.

This poem forms the opening section of a long panegyric,
and the quotation ends at the point where Ibn Hani has
made a skilful transition to introduce his main theme.

Victory

Over you the battle's breeze
Sprinkled sweetest ambergris;
Dawn, unveiling her bright charms,
Succoured your unflagging arms.

So you plucked the fruits of war
That the verdant sword-blades bore,
Ripening upon the tree
Of auspicious victory.

Royal Bounty

My monarch's generosity
Is so abounding, the wide sea
Is spittle in comparison,
The world entire the spume thereon.

Aspiration

So far I set the scope extreme
Of my endeavour and my dream,
I rode the wind, my charger proud,
Intending even to the cloud.

Al-Munfatil
(fl. 11th century)

Enchantress

Friends, hear the story of
My heart's only love:
Lissom is she,
And, as she sweetly sways,
My fond heart obeys
Her witchery.

So sweetly she enchants;
Each firm breast a lance
Pointed at me,
And pointed, guarding yet
Her inviolate
Virginity.

The Mole

There is a little mole
On Ahmad's cheek
That every carefree soul
Aspires to seek.

Red roses fashion an
Enclosure fair,
Yon Abyssinian
Its gardener.

Al-Sumaisir

(*fl.* 11th century)

The Glutton

You gobble all and each
Your fancy bids you cram,
And then abuse the leech
And call his craft a sham.

The fruits of what you sow
You'll gather pretty quick;
The harvest is not slow—
Expect then to be sick.

Your belly is a pot
Collecting day by day
Its noisome food, with what
Dire illness to repay!

Mosquitoes

Mosquitoes are sucking
My blood like sweet wine,
And hey noddy-noddy
They merrily sing.

How nimbly they're plucking,
These minstrels divine!
Their lute is my body,
Each vein is a string.

Al-Kutandi
(*fl.* 12th century)

Elegy for a Dead King

Departs the glorious reign;
Its glories yet remain;
The halo glimmers on,
The moon is—whither gone?

River of Seville

Shining waters of Seville,
Flow you on as sweetly still?
Shall I never more your gleam
Glimpse, not even in a dream?

Nay; 'twas but a lightning, so
Momentarily aglow,
But it faded, and it died,
And in darkness I abide.

Mutarrif
(*fl.* 13th century)

Love's Code

I am a youth as passionate
As you might ever wish to see,
A poet glorious and great,
Sublime in generosity.

Iraq upon her ample breast
Has suckled me with fond desire;
Baghdad has fed me with the best
Refreshment lover could require.

When weary sickness on me lies
Unending, and successive grief
Revisits my unsleeping eyes,
In passion's pangs I find relief.

Such is the code of chivalry
Jamil discovered long ago,
Whereunto others like to me
Have added newly what they know.

The poet acknowledges his indebtedness to the Baghdad
school of poetry, whose fashion he seeks to emulate. He
mentions the famous poet Jamil, of the seventh century,
whose love-lyrics for Buthaina were justly celebrated.

WOMEN

Nazhun
(*fl.* 12th century)

The Blind Man

The poet al-Kutandi challenged the blind al-Makhzumi to
complete the following verses:

If you had eyes to view
The man who speaks with you—

The blind man failed to discover a suitable continuation, but
Nazhun who happened to be present improvized after this
fashion:

All dumbly you'd behold
His anklets' shining gold.

The rising moon, it seems,
In his bright buttons gleams,
And in his gown, I trow,
There sways a slender bough.

Riposte

Ibn Sa'id, Governor of Granada, wrote these lines to Nazhun:

> Your court contains
> A thousand true
> And amorous swains
> In love with you.
>
> Alas, I find
> You give free play
> To all mankind
> Who come your way.

She answered him as follows:

> O Abu Bakr, you occupy
> A place within my heart that I
> Refuse to others; should my breast
> Save by my true love be possessed?
>
> However many there may be
> Who boast they are in love with me,
> All Moslems true give pride of place
> To Abu Bakr of matchless grace.

Nazhun thus turned a pretty compliment upon Abu Bakr's name, which was the same as that borne by the first Caliph of Islam.

Hafsa
(*fl.* 12th century)

The Shield

Vouchsafe to me
A scroll, I pray,
My shield to be
In Fate's affray.

Let your right hand
Inscribe thereon:
'Praise Allah, and
Praise Him alone!'

Exchange

Abu Jaafar the poet was in love with Hafsa, and sent her
the following poem:

God ever guard the memory
Of that fair night, from censure free,
Which hid two lovers, you and me,
Deep in Mu'ammal's poplar-grove;
And, as the happy hours we spent,
There gently wafted a sweet scent
From flowering Nejd, all redolent
With the rare fragrance of the clove.

High in the trees a turtle-dove
Sang rapturously of our love,
And boughs of basil swayed above
A gently murmuring rivulet;
The meadow quivered with delight
Beholding such a joyous sight,
The interclasp of bodies white,
And breasts that touched, and lips that met.

94

Hafsa replied in this manner:

Do not suppose it pleased the dell
That we should there together dwell
In happy union; truth to tell,
It showed us naught but petty spite.
The river did not clap, I fear,
For pleasure that we were so near,
The dove raised not his song of cheer
Save for his personal delight.

Think not such noble thoughts as you
Are worthy of; for if you do
You'll very quickly find, and rue,
High thinking is not always wise.
I scarce suppose that yonder sky
Displayed its wealth of stars on high
For any reason, but to spy
On our romance with jealous eyes.

Guadix

CIVIL SERVANTS

Ibn Farsan
(*fl.* 13th century)

Battle Song

Can I a craven coward be
With lance and sword to succour me,
Or meanly cower, terrified,
With high resolve to lead and guide?

I have no right to fear, because
You are my lion, and your claws
Are very potent to defend
Your cubs, who on your strength depend.

Sing me, my friends, the song of war,
Of steeds that into battle roar;
Their neighing is the tune I seek,
And dripping blood my wine unique.

Cast down my saddle where the stones
Burn in the noonday sun; my bones
Upon that bed are fain to lie,
My tent the pennants swinging high.

Al-Barraq
(1134–1199)

Lyric

Lo, as the thrushes' throats
Throb with their golden notes
The river's silver dress
Shakes in the wind's caress.

The gently cooing dove
(Dost thou not hear, my love?)
Is stirred to ecstasy,
Being so close to thee.

The Inky Mouth

O strange and lovely sight:
A smudge of ink, all staining
A luscious mouth containing
The wine of sweet delight:

Like pitch, a flask of pure
And sparkling liquor lining,
With the moon's crescent shining
Upon a night obscure.

WOMEN

Hamda
(*fl.* 12th century)

Beside a Stream

I sat beside a stream
Of loveliness supreme,
And with my tears expressed
The secrets of my breast.

A mead of emerald
About each river rolled,
And every meadow round
A silver river wound.

Among the shy gazelles
Ran lovely fawns, whose spells
Enslaved my mind, whose art
Bewitching stole my heart.

They lulled their eyes asleep
But for a purpose deep
Which (as true lover knows)
Denies me all repose.

They let their tresses fall
And there, as I recall,
Into the jet-black skies
I saw a moon arise.

The dawn, methinks, bereaved
Of a dear brother, grieved
For so sad loss, and so
Put on the garb of woe.

The poetess refers in the last stanza to the Andalusian custom of wearing white for mourning.

Revenge

And when the scandalmongers strove
Their utmost to destroy our love,
And we could nothing else devise
To take revenge upon their lies;

And since they waged a total war
Against the fair repute we bore,
And few indeed had wit or will
To take our part against their ill;

Then I assailed them with your eyes,
And with my tears, and burning sighs,
And fought against their malice dire
With sword, with torrent, and with fire.

Alcala La Real

POETS

Abu Jaafar
(d. 1163)

Wine, My Love

Ho, bring her hither, happy boy,
For in her presence is my joy,
But (and does love need further proof?)
I grieve when she remains aloof.

I speak upon the wine: when she
Departs, the bowl weeps bitterly,
But when the glass beholds her near
It broadly smiles for the good cheer.

Magian Wine

Wine divinely cool,
Richly worshipful,
Fire and water blent
In one element:

Water made her an
Ardent Magian:
Drunk and dissolute,
We have followed suit.

The Moors diluted their wine with water, and the poet
fancies that the bubbles rising at the mixing are like flames
of fire burning upon a Zoroastrian altar.

Abu Abd Allah

(*fl.* 13th century)

The Water-Wheel

Back arching: so
See her bending low
To suckle with her waters
Earth's lovely daughters.

Her upper half is like
A twanging bow, to strike
With a liquid tide
Of arrows every side.

Or she is a sphere
Celestial, her sheer
Waters meteors hurled
Upon a barren world.

The slim boughs entrance
Her with their swaying dance;
Behold her twirling,
Her sharp swords whirling.

Not of thirst she groans
I think, nor moans
Parched, her shoulder-blade
Drenched in that cascade.

Suppose her then a maid
Singing, and the glade
A drinker, all a throng
Of wine and song:

Her sprinkled dew
Over the dark hue
White gifts to the black
Importuning of lack.

Scurvy Entertainment

Abdul Aziz one day
Invited me to stay:
May Allah, if He please,
Not bless Abdul Aziz!

He poured me wine, the which
Was black as bubbling pitch,
And served (this really hurt!)
Goats' horns for my dessert.

Then came a foul old hag
And offered me a bag
Of raisins, each a mole
Plucked from her withered jowl!

Wine and Citron

Leave the rest, and take the wine
Freshly from the tangled vine;
Gay and amorous is she,
Proof of her virginity.

If the others, praising her,
Aught omitted to repair,
Rhymes I'd string melodious,
Ear-rings fit for Sirius.

Take therewith my golden maid:
She at love has never played,
Of sweet union innocent,
Uninformed of banishment.

Between Pleiades and Earth
Climbs the ladder of her birth;
If you wish to know her sire,
Of green bough and cloud enquire.

Liken her, if fancy bid,
To an ostrich-egg, well-hid,
And the fragrant rushes spread
Cloth of gold, to make her bed.

The lines in italics are a quotation from the pre-Islamic
poet Antara.

Ibn Sa'id
(1210–80)

The River

The river is a page
Of parchment white;
The breeze, that author sage,
There loves to write.

And when the magic screed
Is finished fair,
The bough leans down, to read
His message there.

The Wind

I challenge you to find
A bawd to match the wind,
So skilful to reveal
The charms that most appeal.

The wind knows well to rouse
The chaste and stubborn boughs
And agitate them, till
They stoop to kiss the rill.

So lovers, I have seen,
Make her their go-between,
With joy committing their
Fond missives to her care.

Noblesse Oblige

Refinement is itself refined,
Nobility ennobled, when
A fine and noble lord is kind
And loving unto lesser men.

Although the bough is lifted so
Sublime above the humble ground,
See how he deigns to bow him low
To earth, in courtesy profound!

Strategy

I made myself the friend of all
Who mixed in his society,
That on their succour I might call
Should he prove obdurate to me.

Although the bough be high indeed
And hold himself extremely grand,
A puff of wind with utmost speed
Will send him sweeping to the hand.

The Guardians

Such churlish brutes his guardians be,
Well-schooled in incivility,
Sworn to do battle, when they can,
With every cultivated man.

Whene'er ambitious lover would
Draw nigher to his neighbourhood,
The jealous watchers swiftly rise
And whisk their moon into the skies.

But I have learned a gambit fit
The keenest guardian to outwit,
A stratagem to mollify
The most inexorable spy.

It needs the succour of a shower
For earth to show her guarded flower,
And their hostility relents
When watered with sufficient pence.

The Old Toper

I am reproached for drinking
Although my hairs are white;
If that's your way of thinking,
You are mistaken quite;
The fact that I am hoary
Gives ample grounds to glory
That liquor is my right.

If you will care to listen,
I'll prove what I have said:
When dawn begins to glisten
On night's deep-shadowed head,
See, through the darkness glowing
The cup of twilight, flowing
With wine of richest red!

Changes

How many a supple bough,
My joy of yore, by chance
Malevolent is now
Converted to a lance.

How oft in days gone by
I revelled in a jar
That, now returning, I
Discover vinegar.

Courtship

And when the eyes of love
Crowd round his beauty, he
Puts on the breastplate of
Disarming modesty.

So do our kisses crowd
Importunate to find
His hand, our monarch proud
And pillar of mankind.

Royal Bounty

If panegyric shakes him, then
He scatters gold about;
E'en so the fruit is scattered, when
The bough is shaken out.

Delight your eyes, and ever gaze
Unwearying on his face;
For though it be a sun ablaze,
His hands are clouds of grace.

The Palanquins

Nay, I have ne'er forgotten yet
That day the palanquins were set
Aloft, I fancied them my breast
By deep anxieties oppressed.

And when their curtains, all of red,
Were hoisted over them, I said:
'Yourselves this fatal discord stirred,
And war is kindled by a word.'

The Knights

They might have made an end of death
And slept secure at morning's breath,
Had they not stretched a dusty trail
Along the desert, like a veil.

Their very sword-blades are the same
As they, respecting modest shame,
And, as the foemen's blood they shed,
Their cheeks display a comely red.

Does stubborn enemy suppose
Their spears are little fingers? Those
Same lances soon are fashioning
Each froward heart into a ring.

And of their swords they forge a crown
To press the foemen's temples down
Who, halting in their tracks, express
Involuntary thankfulness.

Did they not fear the guest might stray
Who through the darkness feels his way
Toward their tents, they would bestow
The very stars, and dawn aglow.

The Comely Warrior

His lustrous brow is fair to see
In its fine veil of modesty,
But hard as rock against his foes;
And water e'en from granite flows.

The Virgin

A crimson rose was she
When she came to me,
A golden buttercup
When I gave her up.

I robbed her of the flame
Of her virgin shame;
She melted, and was spilled,
And my hopes fulfilled.

Betrayal

O my friends! I drew
Lovingly to you,
But you cut love's cord
With betrayal's sword.

Heart I poured to heart;
You remained apart;
Wine in water bubbled,
Mind remained untroubled.

Amulet

The jealous breeze, a-shiver
Lest envious glances harm
The beauty of the river,
There writes a magic charm.

The Stolen Penknife

O cunning thief, to rifle
My goods, worth such a trifle
I have no grounds for claiming
Your hand in lawful maiming:

My pens, condemned to splutter,
Vain lamentation utter,
My script, untruly scraping,
Weeps ever for the raping.

In Moslem law the penalty of theft, the striking off of the
offending hand, could not be exacted if the object stolen
was worth less than a specified small amount.

A *Yellow Horse with a Blaze*

Golden is my steed:
I rely on him
In the hour of need,
When the lights are dim.

Like a lamp is he
Scattering its rays
Incandescently,
And the flame his blaze.

A *Yellow Horse with a Blaze*
and a Black Mane

On my charger golden-bright
Oft I set the dust a-flying,
When about the waist of night
Dawn her gleaming belt was tying.

Sleek was he, and high of breed,
Mane of night his neck adorning
(How I gloried in my steed!)
And, between his eyes, the morning.

A *Black Horse with a White Breast*

Blackness behind,
Breast flashing white,
Borne on the wind,
Winged into flight.

Turn you your gaze:
Night is withdrawn:
Lo, he displays
Glorious dawn.

Shem's sons and Ham's,
Vainly reviled,
Peaceful as lambs
Stand reconciled.

All eyes are rapt
In him to see
Beauty's most apt
Epitome.

In the third stanza the poet remembers the legendary
ancestry of the white and black races of mankind, and the
traditional hatred stirred up between them.

Wave Wing

The languid river, like
A bird upon the wing,
Lifts up its wave, to strike
The zephyr flurrying.

The Setting Sun

The sun, about to part,
Sad and sick of heart,
Stretches out his hand, to take
Farewell of the lake.

Sunlight on the Sea

The sun, that bright swan, stoops
Serenely to the west
And, slowly sinking, droops
Its wing on the sea's breast.

The Miser

It pains me less, to stand
And bid my love adieu
Than meanly, cap in hand,
The miser to pursue.

The moon aspires to ape
The sun's refulgent grace,
But vainly: see, agape,
The cracks upon its face!

The furrows on the moon are compared with the wrinkles
upon the miser's forehead when he is asked for charity.

The Crow

If you see the crow, my love,
Inauspicious omen of
Separation imminent,
Say to him: 'O bird, relent,
Or may Allah otherwise
Strike you to the farthest skies!

'How you clamour and you scream
Mournfully in the extreme,
Then you stumble on your way
Showing off your black array,
Satisfied beyond belief
With your cerements of grief!'

Sea of Night

The stars are foam-flecks, white
Upon the sea of night;
The moon, a frigate proud,
Tosses on a cloud.

Wine at Dawn

Rise, and pour me rosy wine,
Dawn aglow at morning shine;
Wine of daybreak, cool to sip,
Crimsons the horizon's lip.

See, the lightnings shake their spears
And the clouds are cavaliers;
Swift their showering arrows come
As the thunder rolls its drum.

And the rivers, rightly pale,
Clothe themselves in coats of mail;
Pardonably do the trees
Sway and shiver in the breeze.

Dawn Song

Pass the winecup; in the east
Heaven holds a wedding-feast,
But your beauty satisfies,
Lovely boy, our greedy eyes.

Lightning's henna'd fingers hurl
Down the sky their drops of pearl;
Heaven's bride her charms displays
Unto dawn's collyrium'd gaze.

The Nuptials

Would you with us had sipped
The wedding-cup of war,
When o'er the warriors dripped
The sweet perfume of gore.

The sun supplied the flowers
And golden moons the night,
The arrows fell in showers,
The swords were lightnings bright.

The 'golden moons' are a reference to the moon-shaped
ornaments worn on the brows at wedding-feasts.

The Tale of Battle

The knights ride off to war,
Flags fluttering in the breeze
Like vultures, circling o'er
The royal enemies.

Their spears will point and prink
The scripture of their swords,
The dust will dry the ink,
And blood perfume the words.

The spears are thought to add the diacritical points of
Arabic writing after the swords have calligraphed the
flowing script in broad slashes.

Love's Storm

And if his sun depart,
The lightning is his heart,
The thunder speaks his fears,
The rains release his tears.

Archery

They are the arrows, and
The chargers are their bows,
The archer is thy firm right hand,
Their targets are thy foes.

Jaen

GRAMMARIANS

Abu Dharr
(d. 1208)

The Oranges

The serried hosts stood man to man,
Determined either side to win,
Here Turk, there Ethiopian,
Their battle-field an orange-skin!

And when the armies 'gan to fight
I never saw a sight so sweet;
The duskies put the blonds to flight,
For they had never known defeat.

But then the pale-faced Turks again
Took heart, and rallied to the fray;
They battled back with might and main,
They fought like heroes all the day.

It is the common rule of war
To fill with tears the watchers' eyes;
But this proved the exception, for
The watchers smiled in glad surprise.

Ibn Faraj
(d. 976)

Continence

And oft I did refrain
From a complacent maid,
When Satan strove in vain
But failed to be obeyed.

She came to me by night;
Her veil was stripped away;
The darkness through her light
Shone radiant as day.

But with all prudence I
Suppressed my lust intense,
That I might practise my
Accustomed continence.

I lay there at her side
Like a young camel, who
Is muzzled, and denied
The breast he would pursue.

In such a garden fair
Naught else for me is meet
Except to stand and stare
And smell the flowers sweet.

For I would not presume
Like cattle left to stray
To trample down the bloom,
And turn the herbs to hay.

Castalla

Ibn Darraj
(958–1030)

Night and Day

And many a dark and youthful night
I struggled through with all my might,
Until his locks were loosed and gray
In the returning light of day.

Which following, a day new-born
A bright and shining boy at morn
I travelled with, until appeared
In gathering gloom his dusky beard.

Ship in Storm

The billows swarmed, impeding
The voyagers who flew
Upon a swan's back, speeding
The stormy waters through.

The ship was lent by morning
A pinion broad and bright;
It fluttered there, adorning
A firmament of night.

Lilies

Lily castles gleam,
Engineered supreme
On their stems to swing
By the hand of spring.

Silver battlements
And, to their defence,
Round the prince his bold
Knights, with swords of gold.

CIVIL SERVANTS

Ibn Abil Khayal
(1072–1146)

Alchemy

Yonder see
Dancing mirthfully
The fire, sleeves shaking
In merry-making.

She laughs with glee,
As her ebony
King of alchemy
Transmutes (behold!)
Her essence into gold.

Almeria

Ibn al-Haddad
(*d.* 1087)

Compliment

Haply you dally
Beside Happy Valley,
Wherefore I clamber
On Indian amber.

Apology

Forgive your faithful friend
Should he by chance offend:
Perfection unalloyed
Too rarely is enjoyed.

All things, by nature's law,
Contain a fatal flaw:
The lantern smokes, despite
Its aureole of light.

Ibn Safar

(*fl.* 12th century)

Flow and Ebb

The river laps the isle,
And complains the while
Hoping she may respond
To his devotion fond.

Suddenly the breeze
Tears his shirt, and flees;
The stream o'erflows his bank
To avenge the prank.

The doves laugh to see
His obesity;
The stream, shamed by the hap,
Fastens up his wrap.

Almeria

Almeria river
(God guard thy gleaming sward),
Viewing thee, I shiver
Like an Indian sword.

O you, beside me striding,
Stay; enjoy with me
This paradise, abiding
Not eternally.

Drink, the while we linger,
To the dove's lament;
Never famed Arab singer
Sang half so excellent.

See, the stream's approving
Murmur seems to rouse
His rapture: moving
Gently, the green boughs

Dance a measure stately
Above the joyous stream;
Their blossoms delicately
Strung (a necklace) gleam

(Hidden, the while drifted
Their sleeves o'er the stream's brow)
Gleam, their sleeves uplifted,
Pearls scattered now.

The breeze rumples
The river into lines;
The silver mail crumples,
The silver sword shines.

The Ship

Ah, but could your eyes
Have seen that ship...The boys
And their ringing cries,
Exultant joy's

Eloquence; a ring
They sat beneath the mast;
Winecup glittering
Hand to hand they passed...

Surely you would have said
The swan, fearing the rude
Tempest, yearning, spread
Her wing over her brood.

Carousal

The drinkers sprawl by night
Beneath the schooner's sail,
Their cup a maiden's bright
Cheek behind a veil.

Fain would the ship conceal
Their secret, but betrays...
As scudding clouds reveal
The sun's glittering rays.

Wine at Morning

Pour me wine: the dew
Crowns the hills anew:
The sunkissed slope discloses
Its cheek, bright with posies.

The dawn's lustre fair
Glitters broadly there,
Like a fountain's jets
Spraying violets.

LAWYERS

Iyad
(1083–1149)

Corn in the Wind

See, in yonder field
The tall cornstalks yield
Before the summer wind,
Bringing to mind

Squadrons streaming out
Of battle in sheer rout,
And the poppies, red
Where the wounded bled.

CIVIL SERVANTS

Ibn Malik
(*fl.* 12th century)

In the Mosque

Slender he was, and fair
As the uprising moon;
I saw him stand to prayer
In the mosque at noon.

And as he bent low
Worshipping, I cried:
'All desire shall so
Be richly satisfied!'

POETS

Ibn Wahbun
(*d.* 1087)

Fate's Malignity

Through the weary nights I strain
My high purpose to attain:
Had my moon but favoured it,
Even Saturn must submit.

In the mirage of the waste
Oft that glitter I embraced;
Oft I glimpsed those sombre eyes
In the overshadowed skies.

Whence derives my wretched luck?
Lo, my arm shrinks not to pluck
At the heights; no idle word
Ever on my lips is heard.

Nay, the fault ascribed to me
Is my fate's malignity:
Shall the sword be held to blame
When the coward muffs his aim?

On Hearing al-Mutanabbi Praised

Ibnul Husain wrote verses eloquent:
Of course: but princely gifts most excellent
Results achieve, and offerings open throats
To make delivery of their sweetest notes.

Exulting in the magic of his tone,
He called himself a prophet: had he known
That you some day would chant his poetry,
No doubt he would have claimed divinity!

Ibnul Husain al-Mutanabbi was the most celebrated
panegyrist in Arabic literature: his name means literally
'the man who claims to be a prophet'. These verses were
addressed to a friend who was reciting and praising
al-Mutanabbi's poetry.

Al-Buqaira
(d. 1135)

The Camomile

When first we parted, she
Wept unrestrainedly;
Fate repenting yet,
In after time we met.

When she was at my side,
'Did those rains' I cried
(Seeing her sweetly smile)
'Produce this camomile?'

The Bow

Ah, my heart grieves
At the hateful bow,
Disloyal so
To the doves in the leaves.

Once warmly befriending,
Now full of spite:
The fates delight
In such an ending.

The Singer

Did I aught else but utter
The praises of your name,
Well content to flutter
In your tree of fame?

If you now deny me
The shelter of your wing,
And no more stand by me,
How then shall I sing?

Ibn Mujbar
(d. 1191)

Departure

White pennant on the wing,
Fondly I watch you rise
In the breeze fluttering,
Wafted by my sighs.

You mark the way he sped,
Vanish he or appear,
As dawn's glittering thread
Proves that day is near.

The poet addressed these lines to a friend marching with
the army into a ravine, and bearing a white pennant.

Red Wine in a Black Glass

I certainly intend
Complaining to my friend
About this glass, alack
Garmented all in black.

I set therein to shine
The sunlight of the wine:
The sun is sinking thence
To darkness most intense.

The beaker, coloured so,
Denies the liquor's glow,
As envious hearts disown
The favours they have known.

Abul Bahr
(1165–1202)

The Abstinent Lover

Beautiful is she,
Beauty all excelling,
A world of witchery
In her gestures dwelling.

Fairer than the moon
Which, her charms so slender
Beholding, craves the boon
Humbly to attend her.

See, the shining grace
Of its crescent golden
Is but her radiant face
In a glass beholden.

On her cheek the mole
Punctuates and stresses
The calligraphic scroll
Lettered by her tresses.

As I lay at night
Nigh to her, night fashioned
Two fires: her beauty bright,
And my sighs impassioned.

Like as o'er his gold
Palpitates the miser,
So yearned I in my hold
Wholly to comprise her.

Yea, I bound her well
In my ardent rapture,
Afraid lest my gazelle
Should escape my capture.

Yet I kissed her not,
Chastity denying
My lust, a furnace hot
In my bosom sighing.

Marvel, if you will:
I, of thirst complaining,
While yet the healing rill
On my throat was raining.

Lorca

NOTABLES

Ibn al-Hajj
(*fl.* 12th century)

Odi et Amo

There is one I love,
Yet I know nothing of
What with his repose
He does, or where he goes.

I detest him, though
I still desire him so,
Like the hoary hair
You hate, yet cannot spare.

Clemency

The more he strives to injure me
The greater is my clemency:
So when the wick is cut, its light
Shines all the clearer through the night.

The Beard

A moon at full: indeed
Your beauty shone unclouded,
Until the nights decreed
Its lustre should be shrouded.

The down appearing, 'So'
I cried, 'fond love removeth,
And yonder monstrous crow
Its sad departure proveth.'

Valencia

CIVIL SERVANTS

Ibn A'isha
(fl. 12th century)

The Apricot Tree

The tree stretched high
Shining as the sky,
Her blossoms raising
Like stars brightly blazing.

A zephyr blew,
And methought it threw
Pebbles at her flowers,
Strewing them in showers.

Did heaven incite
Out of jealous spite
The wind to ravish
Her beauty all too lavish?

Violet

If you deemed his face was fair
When a garden blossomed there,
And the fresh narcissi shed
Fragrance where the roses bled:
Love and cherish it the more
Ardently than e'er before,
Now its charm is sweeter yet
With its fringe of violet.

133

Ibn al-Abbar
(d. 1260)

Jessamine

A garden bright
With jessamine,
Enchanting sight
In dazzling sheen.

Each eye the while
Its shower drips
Provokes a smile
On snowy lips.

And where serene
Each crescent shows,
Its tips between
The twilight glows.

Gilliflower

O give me gilliflowers
(God give you good for those)
Whose perfume all the hours
Of slumber sweetly blows.

The scholar of the night
Converts to day its dusk,
And with his kindled light
Distils the scent of musk.

At daybreak is withdrawn
Its scattered redolence,
As lovers with the dawn
Quit their beloveds' tents.

I love that bloom, by bond
Of common scholarship;
Should scholar not be fond
To press a scholar's lip?

The Wheel

Spun by the weir
The water-wheel turns,
A heavenly sphere
Where star never burns.

Reared o'er the rill
By art, that decrees
Its labouring still
Others to ease.

Freedom to stir
The length of its chains,
A prisoner
Released for his pains.

Rises and sinks
The water: rain
That of ocean drinks
To pour again.

Enchanting indeed:
The saki hastes
With wine for the mead
Himself never tastes.

Al-Dhahabi
(d. 1204)

The Introduction

Most noble Excellence,
Whose earnest eulogy
Based on experience
Good guidance proved to me:

God's recompense be thine
For that thou didst confer,
And may thy star still shine
To guide the wayfarer.

What shaft of lightning glowed
What raincloud to display!
What dawning marked the road
To what refulgent day!

The breeze sweet fragrance shed
To draw my footsteps on:
Unerringly it led
To where the flowers shone.

LAWYERS

Ibn Saad al-Khair
(*fl.* 12th century)

Water

The wheel turns with a will
Its sweet spray to spill
Over the garden, fair
With ripe fruits everywhere.

The lamenting doves
Relate to it their loves,
And the wheel replies
With modulated sighs.

So the lovesick swain
Turns, and turns again,
And weeps, enquiring of
His departed love.

Its eye-ducts are too strait
For its tears in spate,
And so its ribs are split
To loose the flood of it.

Ibn al-Zaqqaq
(*d.* 1135)

Exposure

Gracefully he turns, to pass
Hand to hand the sun-kissed glass,
Slenderly he speeds the cup
Now that dawn is risen up.

And the meadow, swift to please,
Yields us bright anemones,
And the myrtle redolent
Breathes on us its amber scent.

'Where is then the camomile?'
So I asked: and with a smile
He replied, 'Behold the shine
In his mouth, who pours the wine.'

Though the saki long denied
And protested that he lied,
Suddenly he laughed, and there
All the secret was laid bare.

Star Flowers

Pass the cups upon the lawn
Dew-besprinkled this fine dawn;
Morn in undisputed sway
Drives the darkness all away.

Say not that the stars are set:
They are shining brightly yet
And, transported from the skies,
In the meadow now arise.

Night of Bliss

I passed the night most blissfully,
For my true love came to me
And to my breast I held her close,
Bright as morn, till morn arose.

Her arms about my neck were hung
As a sword-belt might be slung,
The while my arms were interlaced
Like a girdle round her waist.

The Portent

The splitting of his cheek
Was no capricious freak,
But thereby God designed
A portent for mankind.

Allah revealed that split,
That we might see by it
As clear as dazzling noon
The way He split the moon.

It is recorded that Allah split the moon in the heavens as
a portent to prove Mohammed's claim to be His prophet.
The poet invents this analogy when his handsome friend's
cheek is wounded.

Frankincense

She sighed, toward me turning
While my breath was burning,
And my brazier hence
Was crowned with frankincense.

Rose-Petals

Rose-petals sprinkled
On the river, wrinkled
By the winds, crossing
The waters, tossing

The waves, like metal
Of breastplate in battle
Hammered and shattered,
Blood-bespattered.

The Bloody Sword

See the sword: on either shank
The blood is flowing,
Like a river, on each bank
Red poppies blowing.

Al-Rusafi
(d. 1177)

The Weaver's Apprentice

Much they reproached me and reviled
Because I loved him so:
'How could you ever have defiled
Yourself with one so low?'

Too well the truth I realise,
And, were it left to me,
I would have chosen otherwise;
But that was not to be.

I love him for his flashing smile,
The fragrance of his sighs,
His sweetest lips, the magic wile
Of his divinest eyes.

My little fawn! His fingers slim
About the spindle move
As swiftly as the thought of him
Provokes my heart to love.

His fingers play as recklessly
With shuttle and with loom
As all the fondest hopes in me
Are trifled with by doom.

His hands embrace the warp, as grope
His feet the woof to set;
He wrestles like an antelope
Caught in a huntsman's net.

The Young Carpenter

When I was told he had been learning
To be a carpenter, I said,
'Perchance he learned his craft by turning
His eyes, to turn a fellow's head!'

Unhappy boughs! They'll soon be rueing
He chose to chop them, this fine spring,
For some are singled out for hewing,
And some are marked for hammering.

Converted to a wooden block! It's
A just reward for roguery
And ever plucking at his pockets
When they were branches on a tree.

The Stream

Poised between its banks, the stream
Serenely curls,
And its limpid waters gleam
Like liquid pearls.

With the noon the great trees thrust
Athwart the flow
Shadows, sombre as red rust
Upon its glow.

Lo, the river in its gown
Of blue brocade
Is a mailclad knight, cast down
In his flag's shade.

Abode Divine

Enchanting night!
O sweet delight
Here upon the lip
Cool wine to sip.

Yonder the sun,
His journey done,
Lays to earth his cheek
Slumber to seek.

A zephyr flirts
With the hills' skirts;
The sky's brow doth gleam,
A burnished stream.

Abode divine!
The night, the wine,
Soothing music of
A cooing dove.

A singing bird,
A green bough stirred:
Darkness leans, to sup
At gloaming's cup.

Al-Nashshar
(*fl.* 12th century)

The Garden

O you, who chide my passion
In so cruel fashion,
When may I hope release
From love, and peace?

Between her cheeks and gleaming
Lips a mole lies dreaming,
A negro who at dawn
Surveys the lawn,

Bewildered which to gather,
Whether he would rather
The roses, or the sweet
Pale marguerite.

Ibn Hariq
(d. 1225)

The Galley

Within its belly dark
The serpent's brood
Still lurks, since Noah's Ark
First rode the Flood.

And as the billows shake
The great ship swung,
From every hole a snake
Flicks out its tongue.

Denia

Ibn al-Labbana
(*d.* 1113)

Patronage

May my life and family
Ransom for my patrons be
Who, whene'er I begged their aid
Against Fortune's ambuscade,
Succoured so my time of trouble
That they left me bending double.

First they made my wings to sprout
Then, when I would shake them out,
Sprinkled them so lavishly
With their liberality
That I have no more the power
To escape their golden bower.

POETS

Ibn Khafaja
(1058–1138)

Lovely Maid

Of a lovely maid I tell:
Sombre eyes of a gazelle,
Throat of hind, and wine-red lip,
Teeth like bubbles sweet to sip.

Drunkenly she swooned and swayed
In her gown of golden braid,
Twinkling stars that interwove
Round the moon, my radiant love.

Passion's hand enveloped us
In his garment amorous
All the night, till it was torn
By the jealous hand of morn.

Treachery

Lo, the copse unbosoms
The glade's mysteries,
For her mouth the blossoms,
For her tongue the trees.

Carousal

Night of pleasure gay!
Full of wine I lay;
Tender was the bed
To my throbbing head.

Thoughtfully the tree
Cast its shade on me;
Bough gave ear to dove
Holding forth on love.

Sickly in the west
Sank the sun to rest;
Thunder muttered loud
Spells to spitting cloud.

The Swimmer

Once (O wonderful)
In a shining pool
I saw a negro swim;
The waters did not dim
The gleaming pebbles spread
On its stony bed.

Now as I observed,
The little pool was curved
Like an eye, and blue
As an eye too;
What was the negro? Why,
The pupil of that eye!

The Roan

And my roan: a brand
Flung out of hand
With elan amazing
To set the battle blazing.

Mid dust and gloom
A pomegranate-bloom,
His ears a myrtle-spray
Pricked to the fray.

The blaze (see it now)
Leaps to his roan brow,
A bubble, laughing up
In the wine-red cup.

Lovely River

Lovely river, spread
On its stony bed,
Sweeter far to sip
Than proud beauty's lip.

Curving through the land
Like a bracelet, and
Fringed with flowers gay,
Heaven's Milky Way.

Overhanging boughs
Sweep about its brows,
Eyelashes that lie
Round an azure eye.

As the zephyrs play
The lithe branches sway:
Sunset's gorgeous beam
Gilds the silver stream.

Abul Qasim
(fl. 12th century)

Rider

Rider, rider hurrying
Ever since the world was born,
Halt a moment at my spring
With the sunset and the morn.

Loiter where my river flows
Sliding like a speckled snake,
And the wizard zephyr blows
Weird enchantments for your sake.

Marj Kuhl
(d. 1236)

Garden at Sunset

Many weary weeks I passed
Waiting for that magic night;
Fate accorded me at last
My impossible delight.

All my highest hopes I gained
Lying in a garden fair,
While the swooning blossoms rained
Scent of amber on the air.

Oh what wonder to behold
Silversmith's and goldsmith's skill:
Silver dirhems, dinars gold
Shone the flowers by the rill.

149

As the ringdoves softly cooed
And the nodding trees leaned down,
Over all the whispering wood
Trailed the sun her golden gown.

And the silver river, wreathed
In the rushes' emerald sheen,
Was a shining sword unsheathed
Glittering on a carpet green.

Ah, its beauty strangely moved
Hearts by passion yet unstirred,
And poetic talents proved
That had never rhymed a word.

And the setting sun grew pale
For no other cause, I guess,
But it felt its heart must fail
Leaving so much loveliness.

Saragossa

Al-Jazzar
(*fl.* 11th century)

Moon of Grace

Neath the hood and cape
That his beauty drape
Shines my moon of grace:
'Ye who love forsake'
Cry his charms, 'O take
Me to your embrace!'

If his garments seem
Coarse, and if ye deem
He is meanly clad,
Yet recall the rose:
Stemmed on thorns, it glows
Beautiful and glad.

Recollect the pitch
Black and brutal, which
Crowns the precious wine,
And remember how
Boxes cheap enow
Harbour musk divine.

Tudela

Al-Tutili
(d. 1126)

Seville

I was bored with old Seville
And Seville was bored with me;
Had the city shared my skill
To invent abusive rhyme,
Rivals in invective, we
Would have had a lovely time.

So at last my weary heart
Could endure no more, and cried
It was time that we should part:
Water in a cloud is cool,
And is much more purified
Than the dribble of a pool.

Battle

Bright as moon serenely burning,
Brave as lion: so he burst
Where the mills of war were turning
And the battle raged its worst.

As I saw the lances gleaming
Round his brow, I was in doubt
If a forest, or a beaming
Halo, circled him about.

Lion Fountain

A lion? No: if I
More closely pry
Methinks that I must own
'Tis but a stone.

Old Leo yonder sits,
So I should say,
And from his mouth he spits
The Milky Way.

Contentment

Leave wealth where wealth is found,
To folk who boast it's theirs:
It is the battleground
Of all superfluous cares.

In avarice and greed
No longer be arrayed:
The sword cuts not, indeed,
Until you bare its blade.

Sacrifice

Accept the sacrifice I made
(If offerings your conscience wake)
Recalling how I disobeyed
The voice of censure for your sake.

Do you remember the long nights
That you and I together spent,
And how you grudged me no delights,
And how I never was content?

POETS

Ibn al-Yamani
(*fl.* 11th century)

Wings of Wine

Heavy were the glasses, though
They were empty when they came;
As I lit in them the flame
Of pure wine, and let it glow

Suddenly they grew so light
That they seemed about to soar,
As the body, gross before,
Flutters with the new-born sprite.

CIVIL SERVANTS

Al-Jaziri
(*d.* 1003)

Forgiveness

When Abu Amir pardoned me
I marvelled at his clemency,
Yet realised that it must soon
Be followed by a greater boon.

For similarly Allah, when
He overlooks the sins of men
To crown His bounty, in a trice
Admits their souls to Paradise.

Al-Lama'i
(*fl.* 10th century)

Night Storm

Yonder drifts a cloud
Limping in the shroud
Of night, as if it were
A footsore wayfarer.

A sudden zephyr swirls
Scattering its pearls:
The cloud hurriedly
Lights a torch, to see.

NOTABLES

Ibn al-Hammara
(fl. 12th century)

The House

You, unique in human kind,
Have a house unique designed:
Lodge therein with equal ease
As the sun in Aries.

Hope could never bid more fair
Than your mortal home to share,
Works no ampler guerdon crave
Than your home beyond the grave.

On the Death of his Wife

Zainab, if you have departed,
Yet the self-same back you rode
Shall transport this broken-hearted
Lodger from his lone abode.

With what ardour should I cherish
Other women for my lust,
While your bloom and beauty perish,
And your charms are turned to dust?

When you fell to the embraces
Of the dusky earth, I cried:
'Lo, the stars have lost their places,
And the sun of love has died.'

156

O most fair and fragile flower
Withering so soon to death,
Did the heavens grudge a shower?
Could the breeze not spare a breath?

Eyelashes

The bird of slumber thought
My pupil was the nest he sought;
He spied the lashes there
And trembled, fearing them a snare.

GRAMMARIANS

Ibn al-Tarawa
(*d.* 1113)

A Saki Refusing to Drink Wine

The grave and reverend divine
Accepts and drinks the cup of wine,
Ensued by all, like him, whose ways
And acts attract the highest praise.

Since our young camel vigour lacks,
His load is shouldered on the backs
Of sturdier workers who, forsooth,
Are somewhat longer in the tooth.

Ibn al-Batti

(d. 1095)

The Hypocrites

I marvel at the gilliflowers
Who shed their perfume all the hours
Of darkness, but their fragrance dies
As soon as dawn is in the skies.

I guess (and the conjecture fits)
That they are natural hypocrites
And, like our moralists, delight
To drink exclusively by night.

Eye and Heart

My eyes and heart:
Each forms, I trow,
The several part
Of some green bough.

Love's flaming woe
The latter sears:
The former flow
With passionate tears.

Pilgrim

I sought you through the world;
Your bounty was my quest;
And mortal dangers swirled
About my hopeful breast.

I braved the billows' shocks,
The ocean's furious ire
Whose blows the very rocks
With awful fear inspire.

As if a comet crashed
From heaven, and there drowned,
And with its tail yet lashed
To foam the waters round.

KINGS

Abu Bakr
(d. 1116*)*

The Sword

My sword I shook
Until
It glittered like a brook,
But frozen, still...

I watched it glow
As bright
As flaming fire, although
Extinguished quite.

Were it not cold
And dead,
It would have burned, or rolled
Away, I said...

Al-Mahdi
(d. 1130*)*

The Preacher

Their shoulders you shook
When they parted; but they
Completely forsook
You, when you went away.

Fine lessons you teach,
But yourself do not school;
Grand sermons you preach,
And remain still a fool.

How long will you whet
Others' swords on your stone,
Continuing yet
Not to cut with your own?

Abur Rabi
(d. 1207)

Petition

Kaaba of the generous hand,
Shrine of bounty and delight,
Sought by Syrian Arab, and
Turkish Ghuzz, and Dailamite!

Blessed pilgrims, who e'en now
Blithely circumambulate
Round your Holy House, and bow
Supplicating at your gate.

Strange it is that they, who hail
From far Syria, fare so well
To behold you, where we fail
Who in your own Mecca dwell.

POETS

Abu Aiyub
(*fl.* 12th century)

The Gift

I thought that it would bring me luck
To send a knife to you,
But my predictions came unstuck:
The omens proved too true.

The dagger is a digger, but
You dug it in my heart:
The cutter cut, the shutter shut,
And I was struck apart.

ASCETICS

Al-Munsafi
(fl. 13th century)

The Skiff

Its legs unlooping
I watched a swimmer glide,
A falcon swooping
By eagles terrified:

An eyeball squinting
Acutely at the sky,
Its oars the glinting
Lashes of the eye.

Colloquy

'Lo, Death has come for thee,
And still thou flounderest in
The ocean of thy sin':
So speaks my soul with me.

'All unprovisioned for
The road....' 'Have done!' I say;
'What provender need they
Who knock at Bounty's door?'

Ibn al-Qabila
(*fl.* 11th century)

Gazelle

The face of a gazelle:
So delicate his skin
That he who looks therein
Beholds his own as well.

I see, as I embrace
My little fawn, how fine
His beauty is: red wine
Seems glowing in his face.

Ah, 'tis not love he seeks:
His only purpose is
That I may glimpse in his
The pallor of my cheeks.

POETS

Al-Hadrami
(*fl.* 13th century)

Departure

How they begrudged him yet
To say farewell, but oh
How generously they let
Him go!

So oft the medicine
For him who suffereth
At last resulteth in
His death.

Beauty's Armoury

As their sides they swayed
They lacked not for lances,
Striking blade on blade
With their killing glances.

Masila

LITTERATEURS

Ibn Rashiq
(*d.* 1064)

Pretences

What makes me disinclined
To visit Andalus
Is the pretentious kind
Of names their rulers use.

The folly that confers
Great names on little scions
Is like the cat, that purrs
To ape the rage of lions.

Rain at Festival

The feast-day wore a frown,
The hail came hammering down:
A glum exchange to see
For smiles, and jollity.

I guess the eager feast
Had come from furthest east
To find you, but it failed
And therefore wept and wailed.

Debauch

All my life I never spent
Such a night of merriment;
Not a sin omitted I
In my after days to try.

Closeted with wine, my love,
Slumber from my eyes I drove,
And my pearl of price untold
Overflowed with liquid gold.

Eagerly I stooped, to kiss
Glowing cheeks in perfect bliss,
As the sparrow stoops, to eat
Hungrily the golden wheat.

The Down

Beauty glittering
In its golden shroud,
Very apt to wring
Rain from barren cloud.

Down-encumbered pride,
Scarce supporting it,
Like a colt untried
Jibbing at the bit.

Hanging head, distressed
At the sight of me
Coming, swiftly dressed
In sweet modesty.

Thinking (but in vain)
That his down should prove
Physic for my pain,
Certain cure for love.

Nay; his cheeks (think I)
Now in down arrayed
Are the thongs, whereby
Hangs his glances' blade.

Continuing Love

Although I turned my head,
Although I little said
To him, of good or ill,
I love my brother still.

I frowned on him, but meant
That I was well content,
As on the winecup now
I gaze with knitted brow.

Malevolence most vile
Oft lurks behind a smile,
And scowls may designate
Quite other things than hate.

Bougie

CIVIL SERVANTS

Ibn al-Qaffun
(fl. 13th century)

Family Tree

High-born child, your brothers twain
In a garden blissfully
Here recline, and pleasures gain
Scarce in Paradise to see:

Large and luscious grapes to eat,
Winking glasses of tart wine,
And, our comfort to complete,
Shelter from a shady vine.

So we sprawl, to little hurt,
Drinking down the blushing maid,
With her mother for dessert,
And her grandam for our shade.

KINGS

Abu Zakariya
(*d.* 1249)

The Spear

My tawny spear is hoar of head
With the dust of battle shed;
Hoary age succeeds in truth
To the verdant bloom of youth.

I reach it out toward my foes
And into their hearts it goes;
Like a rope it sinks, to wrest
Lifeblood from the welling breast.

Bubbling Wine

Spilled into the cup
The wine flames up,
Wreathing it entire
In robes of fire.

Now above the wine
Bright bubbles shine;
Greater wonder eye
May ne'er espy.

See, the wine's aflame;
Yet o'er the same
Dancing hailstones spin,
The wine's own kin.

Abu Zaid

(*fl.* 13th century)

The Army

O wielder of the lance,
Be satisfied: refrain!
Has not your shining glance
Inflicted ample pain?

Although but one you are,
Do you not realise
You carry into war
An army in your eyes?

LITTERATEURS

Al-Husri
(d. 1022*)*

The Breeze

I breathed the blowing breeze
That haply it might ease
My pains, and bring to me
A fragrant air from thee.

Alas, it roused instead
Love's ardour from the dead,
And published far and wide
Love's secret I would hide.

For when fresh winds suspire
O'er an extinguished fire,
They kindle as they blow
The embers, till they glow.

The Tress

A twisting curl
Hung down, to hurl
My heart of bliss
To the abyss.

The sable tress
Of faithlessness
Lent deadly grace
To faith's white face.

Anonymous

My heart doth fly,
Assaulted by
The mallet of
Your tress, my love.

I saw it smite
As black as night,
Its field of play
As white as day.

Ibn Sharaf
(*d.* 1068)

The Protector

Let Noble thy protector be,
Then care not what may chance to thee;
With him thy breastplate have no fear,
Thou art secure from Fortune's spear.

He is as lofty as his name,
His deeds and titles mean the same;
Alike in actions and in speech
He has attained fame's highest reach.

The Lord, the Glorious, the Free,
The Noble: all of these is he,
Describing and connoting him,
His pleonastic synonym.

He ornaments the name of Great
Which other men depreciate;
The sun has opposite degrees
In Libra and in Aries.

173

What lesser rulers make their boast
His glory would disfigure most;
So slender waists are highly prized,
But slender thighs are much despised.

Of him enquire, and in his praise
Be speaking, on his beauty gaze,
And thou shalt find sufficient prize
To fill thy ears, and mouth, and eyes.

The poet puns on the name of his patron Ali, which in
Arabic means sublime.

Chess

I hear men cry on every hand,
'The villains lord it in our land,
They own the wealth we beggars need,
And horses of the noblest breed.'

'Time marches on': so I exclaim.
'Fate plays at chess, and Fortune's game
Goes on as it has ever been:
The pawn may yet become a queen.'

Concert

Thanks for the lovely time
We spent with you last night;
The music was sublime,
The programme a delight—

The singing of the flies,
Mosquitoes on the flute,
And, as the big surprise,
The fleas that danced to suit.

POETS

Al-Fata al-Kafif
(*d.* 1095)

White for Mourning

If it is the use
In Andalus
For mourning to wear white,
It is but right.

See you not, in ruth
For perished youth
The white hairs I now
Wear on my brow?

Ibn Faddal
(*fl.* 11th century)

The Young Pilgrim

'Why so young, and set
On the Pilgrimage?
Wait a little yet,
Till you come of age.

'But if you intend
So determinedly,
When you thither wend
Kiss the Stone for me.

'And if there you aim
Pebbles, cast them true
At those hearts that came
Ne'er in flight to you.'

175

'Leave me!' he replies,
'That in Zemzem then
I may cleanse my eyes
Of the blood of men.'

The poet refers to various ceremonies connected with the pilgrimage to Mecca. The last stanza refers of course to the lovers' heartblood shed by the lances of the handsome boy's eyes.

CIVIL SERVANTS

Al-Ghassani
(*fl.* 13th century)

Roses

Roses, roses fresh and fair
Shining on the summer air
In their jackets crimson bright
And their tunics snowy white.

These in virgin whiteness are
Dazzling like a lustrous star,
Those in crimson splendour show
Radiant as twilight's glow.

Others have a golden gleam
In their centres, that would seem
Grains of sesame, heaped up
In the middle of their cup.

Eclipse

When the moon's immortal glow
Is eclipsed (and there is no
Other star in all the skies
Such catastrophes befall)
'Tis as if some lovely lass
Spies her image in a glass
And, in envious surprise,
Turns the mirror to the wall.

Bona

CIVIL SERVANTS

Al-Qalami
(*fl.* 12th century)

Ramadan

Holy Ramadan,
Season sanctified,
More dear to Allah than
Every other tide!

Yet to mortal man
(What is hardly right)
Thou dost unkindly ban
Drunkenness' delight.

Glass that clinks on glass
(O divinest bliss)
Mouth pressed to mouth: alas
That denied and this.

So I swear, by those
Who devotedly
Each moment as it goes
Do honour unto thee

As by all their prayers
Offered up to God,
Both single and in pairs,
The even and the odd

Glad am I in heart
Now to see thee die,
Although with thee a part
Of my life goes by.

NOTABLES

Sharaf al-Din
(*d.* 1247)

Fragment

·Amid the shining swords and lances
None so braggingly advances,
None so bravely, no, not one
As Abdul Mumin, Ali's son.

The Water-Cooler

Like the fire it came to birth
In the bowels of the earth,
Water easefully to bear
In a cool, refreshing air.

In its depths, for our delight,
The four opposites unite,
Blending far more perfectly
Than our frail humanity.

Lo, its little ones are tied
Ever closely to its side
Like the desert cow, that rests
With her calves about her breasts.

When the barren udder fails,
Yonder maiden yet regales
And refreshes one and all
With her flow ambrosial.

Let the eye observant see
Her most shapely symmetry,
Let the contemplative glance
Note her height, and elegance.

So the Pleiades on high
Hang suspended in the sky,
As with threads of cotton tied
To a rocky mountainside.

Loose her from her prison bars
And she flashes with her stars,
Swooping like the Gemini
To delight the watcher's eye.

The poet describes the Egyptian water-cooler, a tall vessel
with cups attached about its neck. In the first stanza he
employs the literary elegance of mentioning the four
elements. The verse in italics is a quotation from Imrul Qais.

POETS

Ibn al-Talla
(*fl.* 11th century)

The Artichoke

Lovely little daughter
Born of earth and water:
Still her excellence is
Barred by the defences
Avarice erects
Hopeful hearts to vex.

With her flesh so white,
Guarded in the height
Of her tower surging,
Like a Turkish virgin
Bashfully she peers
Through her veil of spears.

POETS

Ibn Qadi Mila
(*fl.* 11th century)

Fruit Tree

When bosoms quivering
On slender bodies swing,
Patience, your day is o'er:
Forbearance can no more.

I love those boughs to see
That sway so gracefully;
Especially they suit
My taste, when hung with fruit.

The Lute

God ever bless the earth
That brought your tree to birth:
Its branches thrived indeed,
And fruitful was its seed.

Birds sang on every bough
When it was green; and now,
Though withered through and through,
Fair maidens sing thereto.

Abul Arab
(1031–1112)

The Gift

You gave to me a camel black
And, loaded on the camel's back,
A load of silver glittered there
The camel struggled well to bear.

Now wonder at me, if you will,
For was it not more wondrous still
How, nourished by your hand, I strode
Bearing the camel and the load?

The poet was made the gift of an ebony statue of a camel
loaded with silver coins.

Ibn Hamdis
(*d.* 1132)

Flowing Stream

The surface of the flowing stream
Is polished by the prying wind,
Resolved to publish, it would seem,
The secrets hidden in its mind.

The jagged pebbles gash its flanks,
And as the waters swell again
And ever o'er the river's banks
It murmurs fretfully in pain.

As if a serpent, terrified
Beneath the bubbles as it sleeps,
Awakens suddenly, to slide
Impetuously in its deeps.

Early Pleasure

Rise up, rise up in haste
The dawn's delights to taste;
Mount swiftly, shining boy,
The fiery steed of joy.

Make speed, before the sun
Is risen, and begun
The dewy wine to sip
From every poppy's lip.

Night Visitor

My love came to me, when night
Spread her wings across the skies:
Welcome to thee, sun most bright
Tarrying not for dawn to rise!

Moon in Eclipse

Whenas the swarming flood of night
Was ebbing from the sky
The moon, eclipsing, lost the light
Of half its eye.

The moon a blacksmith's mirror seemed
That, furnaced more and more,
Glowed, till the fiery crimson streamed
Its blackness o'er.

Water-lilies

Drink by the pool
Where shines the beautiful
Water-lilies' sheen,
Crimson on green.

The blossoms break
The mirror of the lake,
And adroitly aim
Their tongues of flame.

Ibn Abi Bishr
(*fl.* 12th century)

Sunshine

When the sun was sinking
We set ourselves to drinking
A sun, that glittered bright
Until the rising light

Of dawn, above the river
Thrusting, struck, to quiver
Like lances with their points
Stuck in the armour's joints.

INDEX OF POETS

INDEX OF POETS

INDEX OF
FIRST LINES

INDEX OF FIRST LINES

INDEX OF FIRST LINES